D1562017

ADVANCED SCOUTING TECHNIQUES

JUDD COONEY

NORTH AMERICAN HUNTING CLUB
Minneapolis, Minnesota

COMPLETE DEER HUNTING LIBRARY

HS

NORTH AMERICAN HUNTING CLUB

Mike Vail	Vice President, Products and Business Development
Steve Perlstein	Book Products Development Manager
Dan Kennedy	Book Development Coordinator

This book was originally published by Derrydale Press, Inc.

All photos in this book by Judd Cooney, except the following:
Page 66   Max Johnson
Page 118 Steve Perlstein

ISBN 0-914697-82-X

Printed in the United States of America
This book was printed on acid-free paper with 10 percent
post-consumer recycled content.

TABLE OF CONTENTS

EDITOR'S FOREWORD

With this book we come to the twelfth volume of our Whitetail Secrets series. I've learned a great deal from each and every author, and I'm sure you have as well. And I know you'll find that equally true with Judd Cooney's volume on scouting.

I've known Judd for quite some time, and he's quite a guy. Actually, we have a great deal in common when it comes to whitetails. Judd has lived most of his life in western Colorado. Now, Colorado is a great whitetail state . . . but on the east side. So, like me, Judd hasn't grown up with whitetails in his backyard. He's had to scout them out first from afar and then up close and personal . . . and he's done it well. Well enough that he's become an extremely successful whitetail outfitter.

But that's not unusual with Judd Cooney, a man of many accomplishments in the hunting world. He's been a very successful outfitter for black bear, deer, elk, and other western species for decades—also an extremely accomplished bowhunter in his own right. His knowledge and experience eventually led him into a very successful outdoor writing career over the last decade or so. When Judd Cooney gets into something, he gets into it with both feet. He hunted whitetails for himself all over the country, but that wasn't enough, so he wound up starting a whitetail outfitting business in Iowa, the state that has emerged as one of the top all-time big-buck areas. His name was in darn near every outdoor magazine, but that, too, wasn't enough; he just took over as President of the Outdoor Writers Association of America. And believe me, that's a tough and thankless job I wouldn't want . . . I admire a man like Judd Cooney who was willing to interrupt his own career to head up such a group!

Let's see, hunter, outfitter, writer. Oh yes, there's one more professional accomplishment of Judd Cooney's that I need to mention: He's every bit as handy with a camera as he is with a gun or bow. In fact, this series simply couldn't have existed without him. Most of us poor dumb writers just aren't worth a darn with a camera. I knew that, and I knew I'd need some extra photos as I went through the task of preparing each manuscript for publication. This series has featured the work of a number of very fine photographers: Mike Biggs, Charlie Alsheimer, Ian McMurchy. But Judd Cooney has been our primary photographic contributor and there's a reason for that. When I asked him to send a few photos he sent two big boxes of more than 500 sharp, clear black-and-white photos . . . along with several hundred slides! No matter what I needed to help illustrate an author's point, Judd Cooney had a photo that fit. Like me, Judd Cooney doesn't have whitetails in his backyard, but he's sure spent a lot more time around them than I have!

Taking pictures, by the way, is also scouting, making Judd Cooney uniquely qualified to share his secrets to "Advanced Scouting Techniques."

Craig Boddington
Paso Robles, California

CHAPTER ONE

THEORY OF SCOUTING

Scouting is defined by Webster's dictionary as: "to explore an area to obtain information" (as about an enemy, or in our case an adversary, the whitetail deer). This short, concise definition is a gross understatement when it comes to scouting for whitetail deer, whitetail bucks in general, and record-book whitetail bucks in particular.

You may not realize it, but scouting is the key ingredient that will ultimately control the success or failure of every single whitetail hunt in which you'll ever participate. It doesn't matter whether you're bowhunting in Alabama, rifle hunting the rolling hills and bush country of Alberta in 30-degree below-zero weather, muzzleloader hunting the timbered ridges of Pennsylvania, or shotgun hunting the cornfields of Iowa. Scouting, or the lack thereof, will play a major role in the success or failure of your hunt.

You can be hunting in your grandma's apple orchard behind the barn a mile from your house, or traveling to the rolling hills of Illinois on a do-it-yourself hunt, or spending big dollars to hire the best outfitter in Montana or Saskatchewan. If you or your outfitter and guide don't do some serious and intelligent scouting and gain as much information as possible on the whitetail population, including its habits and idiosyncrasies pertinent to the area you are going to be hunting, your chances of success are going to be greatly diminished.

Scouting is simply looking . . . but the more you know what to look for and how to use the information the more successful you will be.

You can't drive your vehicle up to the edge of a cornfield on opening morning of the gun season and sit on the hood with a reasonable expectation of seeing a deer, unless you have done a minimum of scouting and: (1) Knew the cornfield was there; (2) Knew there were, or at least had been at some time, deer in the vicinity of the field. You can't hang a

Tony Knight of Knight Muzzleloaders with a fine whitetail. Luck is okay, but good scouting is a more sure way to a fine buck like this.

treestand over a scrape, food source, or trail unless you scouted out these locations and found a useable tree within range for your stand location. You can't even book an out-fitter to do all the critical scouting for you without doing a bit of scouting on your own, to locate his name and address from somewhere or someone. The name of the game is scouting, pure and simple!

According to Dan Bertalan, book author, host of the "Bowhunting America" TV show, and freelance writer specializing in bowhunting, and in particular whitetail hunting articles, "You might have all the pieces of HOW and

Looking for deer is an important part of scouting, but often locating concentrated sign is even more valuable.

'WHEN' to tag a trophy whitetail buck, but without the exact 'WHERE' you'll still be unsuccessful. Proper scouting is the key to unlocking the door to 'WHERE' and the success that awaits you."

Scouting and hunting are almost one and the same

Rubs are important signposts at any time of the year, since bucks will often return to rubs year after year.

thing. It's often difficult to draw a line as to when you are scouting and when you are hunting. Scouting is basically seeking a place to hunt and hunting could easily be thought of as scouting for an animal to shoot or a place to

Learning what foods deer are eating at various times of the year is a constant and ongoing principle of savvy scouting.

shoot from. The main differentiation would be that most pure-form scouting takes place outside the season. During the legal hunting season scouting and hunting mingle so much that one would only get thoroughly confused trying to mentally separate the two, so let's just consider them an inseparable and vital combination once the season opens and leave it at that.

The higher your personal expectations as to the quality relating to antler dimensions (every whitetail deer is a trophy animal in my estimation) of the trophy whitetail you are hunting, the more important thorough and proper scouting techniques become. If you are scouting for a place to just kill a whitetail deer, be it buck, doe, or fawn, you may get by with a minimum of scouting effort a day or two before your hunt takes place. If you or the game laws in your hunting area limit your choice to an antlered deer only, you are going to have to expend a bit more effort in narrowing down your hunting area to locations where you are most likely to get within shooting distance of a buck. If you're limiting your choice to a whitetail buck in the 2½ year or older category, you had better plan on spending some serious time and effort in the field prior to your actual hunt, locating and studying the local deer population to find a buck worthy of your opening morning hunting efforts. If your desires run toward adding a Pope & Young or Boone & Crockett–class whitetail buck to your big game collection, you had better plan on making your scouting efforts a year-round project and expending a lot more effort in scouting than you do in actually hunting. Even if you plan on hunting with a professional outfitter or guide, you had better do some serious scouting to locate the best individual in the best buck producing area, where your chances of scoring on one of these "super" bucks will be as high as humanly possible.

There's an old saying: The harder you work, the luckier you get! Truer words were never spoken when it comes to scouting for whitetails.

CHAPTER TWO

DESKTOP SCOUTING

If you're at all like me you probably have a sincere aversion to research, office work, correspondence, and anything else that is liable to keep you housebound when you could be outdoors in the fresh air and sunshine. However, quite possibly the most important aspect of your scouting is going to be carried out under the roof of your house.

A major part of intelligent scouting is gathering pertinent information on your hunting area as well as on the deer that roam the neighborhood. One of the easiest and most efficient ways to gain considerable knowledge about your hunting grounds can be accomplished during the off-season months, in the comfort of your own home. Any whitetail hunter serious about being successful should not only be intimately familiar with every square yard of his chosen hunting area but have a very thorough knowledge of the surrounding area. You may well be able to scout out your hunting area during various times of the year but how about the surrounding property that belongs to someone else and is off-limits to your on-the-ground scrutiny? Often knowing the key land features of neighboring properties and how they can effect deer movements onto your hunting area during various seasons and under varying circumstances can be vital to your success. The best way to accomplish this during the off-season is by utilizing U.S. Geological Survey maps and aerial photos. These easy-to-

Every whitetail hunter wants to put himself or herself in this picture, but rather than daydream about it, you can scout for it from the comfort of your easy chair.

use maps and photos can give you an extremely accurate overall view of your hunting area and as much of the surrounding terrain as you deem necessary.

The first step in outfitting yourself with a set of U.S.G.S. maps and aerial photos is to contact the U.S. Geological Survey Information Services Office, Box 25286, Denver,

While true trophy areas are scarce, literally every whitetail state has areas or units that produce plenty of nice bucks like this one.

CO 80225. Phone: 1-800-USA-MAPS or 303-202-4700. Order a U.S.G.S. state map catalog and an index map of the state or states you are interested in. Once you get the index it's easy to pinpoint the area of primary interest and order specific maps from the catalog that will cover these sections. The U.S.G.S. also provides excellent county maps for some states in a scale of 1:50,000 or 1:100,000. These county maps are not available for all counties in all the states, but if you are fortunate enough to find them for your hunting area they are extremely useful, especially for locating and scouting out new hunting properties.

The most useful maps will be the standard quadrangle topo maps in a scale of 1:24,000 where 1 inch on the map represents 2,000 feet on the ground. These maps are 22" x 27" and show everything but a buck's beds, rubs, and scrapes. The catalog will also list topo map dealers in your state where you can buy or order the same maps across the counter.

To order aerial photos of your specific hunting locale, outline the area you need photo coverage of on a U.S.G.S. map or a good copy of the map and send the marked map or maps to: U.S. Department of Agriculture, Aerial Photo Field Office, Box 30010, Salt Lake City, UT 84130. Phone: 801-975-3503. The map section will research your photo request and advise you what they can provide in the way of photo coverage, the date the area was last flown and photographed, sizes available, and prices. These are available in either standard black-and-white 9½" x 9½" photos, or 38" x 38" photos. Shipment of your specific photos will take from four to six weeks from initial order date. The county extension office in the county seat where you hunt may also be able to provide you with photocopies of aerial photos of your hunting area.

To alleviate the pain of trying to use bulky, easily dam-

Desktop scouting is simply information gathering, and hunters who have been in a given area are a prime resource.

Aerial photos are a great tool for getting an overall view of your hunting area and locating key points such as rubs, scrapes, travel corridors, etc.

aged U.S.G.S. map sheets at home or in the field, I take a set of maps that covers my complete hunting area, which in the case of our Iowa hunting operation involves three counties and portions of 12 different U.S.G.S. maps, and mount them on a cloth backing called Chartex. By cutting the maps into approximately 12" x 12" sections, laying them out on the Chartex with a ¼"–½" space between sections and ironing them onto the adhesive-backed muslin, I have a complete map of my entire hunting area that will fold into a compact, portable, 12" x 12" packet. My wife sewed up a canvas carrying case that protects my U.S.G.S. maps and a number of aerial photos while I am carting them around in the field and yet keeps them readily accessible.

SCOUTING FROM TOPO MAPS AND AERIAL PHOTOS

The first step in using topo maps and aerial photos for desktop scouting is to get a comfortable familiarization with them in relationship to the actual lay of the land in your hunting area. First off locate and outline the property boundaries of your hunting area regardless of whether it's private or public land. Next find and mark all the major landmarks in your hunting area such as farm buildings, ponds, roads, fields or food plots, creeks or streams, peaks, swamps etc. It's a good idea to further expand this procedure to include the lands adjacent to your hunting area. Knowing the lay of the land on the adjoining properties could play a major role in figuring deer movements onto or off your hunting territory during various times of the season or under certain circumstances and could play a key role in your future hunting ventures.

While you are studying your topo maps and aerial photos you might run across a section of countryside that just screams, "ideal whitetail country!" Any whitetail hunter worth his salt is always on the lookout for new hunting area and when you find such an area one of the first things you'll need to accomplish is to find out the land ownership status so you can attempt to get permission. An indispensable item for this is a Farm & Home Plat Directory usually available from the county extension office in the county seat where you are hunting. This directory shows the land ownership status and owner's name for all the land in the county and can prove invaluable in your search for new hunting area.

Whether or not you're familiar with your intended hunting area, studying a topo map and aerial photos will give you a look at the landscape from a broad overview and provide a much better overall perspective of your hunting area and the surrounding country. Unfortunately the U.S.G.S. doesn't locate and provide map symbols for whitetail feeding areas, bed grounds, travel corridors, funnels, saddle crossings, or rub and scrape lines. These specific terrain features are all on your topo map and aerial photos. You just have to ferret them out and mark them for future use.

Feeding areas such as corn, oat, barley or soybean fields, alfalfa patches, apple orchards, and clover plots can be delineated and marked on your maps and photos. From there you can search out the more obvious travel routes, and funnels where a section of woods or brushy corridor runs from one feeding area to another and narrows down or restricts a deer's options for traveling in protective cover. Saddles in ridge lines separating one feeding area from another are also good spots to mark on your maps for checking on the ground later during the spring scouting sessions. Large areas of timber and brush, gullies, weed patches, sloughs, old abandoned farmsteads, or any other small secluded

MENTION YOUR FARM & HOME PLAT & DIRECTORY

The many businesses and professional firms who
through their advertising have made the plat & directory
possible for you . . . when buying mention your
"Farm & Home Plat & Directory" to them.

T-85-N **LAKE PLAT** **R-46-47-W**

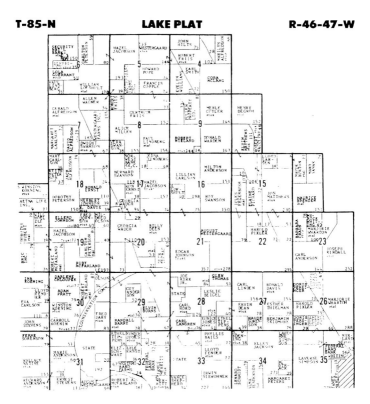

*A county plat directory will give you ownership status of all private
land in the county.*

A lot of productive scouting can be done from a topo map at home. Then, on the scene, use the map to verify your suspicions about likely deer locations.

areas that are out of sight or isolated from roads and off the beaten people path are just the sort of locations that a big buck will seek out during the season when he has been pressured. Any such area that catches your attention on your maps or photos should be noted and marked for further on-the-ground study during the coming year's scouting.

You can spend hours going over your aerial maps and photos and not a minute will be wasted. The more you use them and correlate them to what is actually on the ground the more efficient you will become at second-guessing that trophy buck and the better you will be at getting into position on him before he even knows that is where he is headed. By keeping good notes and making constant use of aerial photos and topo maps to mark the locations of rubs, scrapes, bedding areas, major travel corridors, funnels, saddles, and such during your actual hunting endeavors you should find definite patterns emerging that will make second-guessing those mature bucks a bit more certain.

CHAPTER THREE

SCOUTING EQUIPMENT

We've already determined the importance of scouting as an indispensable information-gathering medium for whitetail hunters that just might be the most significant element of your fall whitetail hunting ventures. Proper scouting techniques can provide you with a wealth of information that will let you plan and execute your fall hunt with confidence and enhance your chances of ending the season with a freezer full of meat and a set of antlers for your den. Proper technique is definitely an important aspect of your scouting ventures to be sure, but equally important is proper scouting equipment.

Everything, from the truck you drive into the countryside to the footgear you wear while hiking the hills, plays an important role in your year-round scouting outings and can increase the efficiency and effectiveness of your scouting or detract from it, as the case may be.

A thorough discussion of vehicles and their uses in scouting would take a book in itself and still not cover all the bases so I'll just stick to some of the things I've learned about vehicle use over the years. A four-wheel-drive vehicle is by far the most useful equipment-hauling, blind, and optics tripod combination available. A 4x4 can get you farther off the beaten path and will keep you in the field longer during inclement weather and terrible terrain con-

Good binoculars and spotting scope can make glassing from a vehicle an easy proposition.

ditions that will bring a two-wheel-drive vehicle to a standstill. Over the years I've made extensive use of both the enclosed-interior 4x4s such as the Bronco, Blazer, and Suburban, as well as pickups. I prefer a pickup for hauling equipment such as treestands, ladders, blinds, four-wheelers, snowmobiles, etc. My Suburban is great for hauling gear that needs to be kept out of the weather and also serves as a protected place to sleep on many scouting and photo trips. Scouting from your vehicle is often the least intrusive method you can use. A whitetail will put up with a vehicle several hundred yards away much more readily than it will a person standing or walking the same distance.

Just because you have four-wheel drive doesn't necessarily mean you can ride roughshod over private land without giving any thought to the damage you might do. I've met many landowners that have closed their land to hunters because of the damage caused by 4x4's. A set of ruts

Good binoculars are essential for scouting year-round and should provide a lifetime of use.

The GPS (Global Positioning System) will store locations of scrapes, rubs, travel corridors, etc. as waypoints that can be collated during the off-season and added to your maps and notebook.

gouged out of a steep hillside or across a spring-soft pasture or field, by a careless, unthinking hunter can lead to serious erosion and "NO HUNTING" signs on the gates. When you get permission for your scouting and hunting ventures on private property make sure you get a firm understanding from the landowner as to rules governing the use of vehicles on the property. Another tip for keeping your good relations with the property owners on whose land you are hunting and their neighbors is to keep them informed as to what vehicles you will be using while you are on their land. If I'm driving by a farmhouse on a regular basis in my comings and goings from a hunting area, I will try to stop and let the farmer or his wife know who I am, what I am doing, and the vehicles I will normally be driving. This does much to alleviate their curiosity about the unknown and may just give you an in for getting hunting permission in the future. It's the little courtesies, often overlooked, that end up costing us in the long run.

Four-wheelers, either the 2x4s or 4x4s are another great tool for some serious nonintrusive scouting on a year-round basis. These handy, "go anywhere" outfits are popular with fishermen, hunters, campers, and weekend warriors. Fortunately they are also extremely popular as a working tool for ranchers, farmers, timber cruisers, game and fish personnel, and deer hunters. That's definitely a plus when it comes to utilizing them for scouting and/or for actually transporting hunters into the hunting area. The deer are accustomed to the sounds of these machines burbling around the woods and fields and probably won't go into a total panic when they hear the sound of one in their area during the middle of the day. In large tracts of public land where four-wheeling is legal, you can cover a vast amount of country on back roads and trails checking for well-used crossings, big tracks, scrapes, and rub lines without leaving a smidgeon of scent or disturbance on the ground. Once you locate an area with lots of fresh sign you can really put your scouting techniques to work.

The four-wheeler's light weight and large, low-pressure tires leave a low-impact footprint-making it ideal for travel in areas where minimum ground or vegetation damage is imperative. Four-wheelers (especially, four-wheel drives) are excellent for traveling through heavy bush, timber, swamp, or muskeg areas to get off the beaten path where there are fewer hunters and less wary deer. In such places the deer aren't as accustomed to the sounds of machines, so don't overdo its use. Use your four-wheeler to get back into the area as unobtrusively as possible and then park it and do your serious scouting on foot. Another advantage of scouting and actually making use of a four-wheeler for hunting is the fact you don't leave scent on the ground for a sharp deer to detect. In my hunting and guiding operations I often prefer to ease a hunter up to a blind or treestand with a vehicle or four-wheeler. I'll drive right up to the treestand or blind, let him exit quietly out and then drive off. A vehicle traveling across a meadow, harvested field, or down a back road disturbs deer far less than a human walking or sneaking on foot. A deer spotting a vehicle headed its way will usually just get back in the timber and let it pass. After a few minutes the deer will usually settle down and continue with its normal activities. This may not be the case in areas where there is substantial night hunting and poaching. If a deer spots a hunter sneaking to his stand in the predawn darkness or scents the passage of such an intruder he will more than likely vacate the area in short order and let every deer in the area know about it. The only scent trail a hunter traveling to a stand or blind in a vehicle or four-wheeler is going to leave is from the vehicle to the stand. This minute amount of scent and short trail is a lot less likely to be detected by a deer's sensitive nose than the scent trail of a hunter walking a quarter mile or more to the stand.

Another method of scouting an area without disturbing the area and spooking deer is by horseback. There are many large tracts of superb whitetail habitat across the nation that just scream for the use of a good saddle horse for efficient, low-impact scouting. You can cover a lot of ground on horseback, locating and working out scrape and rub lines, work, your way through bedding areas, traveling and locating the entrance and exit trails, and following well-used trails to hidden feeding grounds or trees. With a little care such as wearing clean canvas chaps, rubber boots, and gloves you can do all this and more without disturbing or alerting the local deer population to your intrusion or intentions by leaving little or no scent. This next fall I am going to be giving some serious consideration to making a lot more use of a horse or two for our Iowa whitetail operation. I can't think of a better way to transport a hunter into a hot buck area and ease him into a treestand, pit or ground blind without leaving scent or spooking deer.

It's impossible to think about serious scouting at any time of the year without thinking about good optics. A good pair of binoculars is essential to effective scouting of any type. There is a profusion, or I should say confusion, of binoculars on the market that range in price from $10 to $2,500.

I'm always amazed when an ardent whitetail hunter shows up in hunting camp with an "el cheapo" pair of miniature binoculars that probably couldn't distinguish between a bull elk and a doe whitetail at 500 yards, even in the bright sunshine of midday. When asked about this sorry state of optical affairs, they usually state emphatically,

"I do all my whitetail hunting in heavy cover and at short distance so why do I need an expensive pair of hefty binoculars to haul through the woods or up into a treestand with me?" Scouting! That's why!

Without a decent pair of binoculars it's often tough to distinguish between an average buck and a "boomer" buck in the early morning or late evening light these antlered phantoms seem to prefer. I wouldn't think of going out scouting without toting a pair of the best quality binoculars and spotting scope I could afford. I'd much rather let my eyes do the walking; it's a lot less tiring, I can cover a lot more country in less time and I don't make noise or leave a bit of scent to spook or alert a sly, old buck.

Good binoculars are the best combination of magnification, image quality, light-gathering ability, size, weight, and durability. Binocular quality is often hard to judge across the counter in a sporting goods store but a first-class binocular indisputably reveals its worth during low-light conditions and periods of extended use. Glassing with a set of low-quality binoculars for a prolonged period of time will leave your eyes feeling like somebody poured sand and salt in them. Determining the trophy aspects of a buck under low light situations with poor quality glass lenses will leave you mumbling to yourself and cussing the guy that sold you the glasses. The durability of a quality binocular shows up dramatically during extreme field conditions of heat, cold, moisture, bumps, and jolts.

One of the most important aspects of a good scouting binocular is its twilight factor. This is a complicated term calculated by taking the square root of the binocular's magnification multiplied by the objective lens diameter. The higher the twilight factor, the better the binocular's light-gathering ability for low-light conditions and the easier it will be for you to locate deer and judge a buck's headgear

The Trailtimer is the simplest and most economical of the trail monitors that will give you the time and direction of a passing deer.

during low-light conditions. A good pair of binoculars for hunting and serious scouting should have a twilight factor of at least 15 or higher. Such things as purity of the glass used in the lenses and prisms and the quality of the reflection-reducing lens coatings that minimize unwanted reflections and maximize light transmission are all factors that affect the overall brightness and sharpness of the image you see under adverse scouting conditions.

I also prefer central-focusing binoculars, where you can fine-tune both oculars simultaneously rather than individual-focus binocs where you adjust each ocular separately. Center-focus glasses can be easily adjusted to your individual eyesight requirements by independently adjusting the right ocular. One-handed fine tuning is easily accomplished with center-focus binocs and can be a real pain with individual-focus glasses.

Stay completely away from the "auto focus" or "stay focus" type-binoculars that do not have focusing adjustments. Their price and ease of use may sound appealing but they are primarily designed for birders and people who only use binoculars sparingly. These binoculars force your eyes to do the focusing or adjusting. After a serious scouting session, where your eyeballs are zooming in and out, focusing and refocusing constantly over a couple, hours' time, they're going to feel like they've been sandpapered.

For general scouting and hunting I prefer a set of 7X binoculars and make use of a set of 10X glasses when I am glassing from a vehicle or can make use of a good solid rest. The lower the magnification the easier they are to hold steady offhand.

My vocation as a guide and outfitter necessitates locating deer and other critters before they spot me or my clients. Good optics are a vital part of that function and I want the best that I can afford as they are the most utilized and in-

A buck headed for Trailmaster monitor on tree at left.

dispensable tools in my hunting arsenal. A good set of binoculars is certainly not cheap, but a pair of quality glasses will usually provide a lifetime of excellent service and use. I never have figured out the rationale of a serious whitetail hunter who will spend $400. or more on a new bow that will usually only last a few years and then buy the cheapest pair of binoculars available and expect them to give a lifetime of quality use. Good binoculars may well have more to do with the success or failure of his whitetail hunting ventures than his bow.

My personal choice in binoculars has been narrowed to two or three of the sharpest, brightest, and most rugged models I have been able to find. For years I have dangled a pair of Swarovski rubber-armored 7x42s around my neck on whitetail and other big game hunts across the country. This past hunting season I started switching back and forth between the 7x42s and a pair of Nikon SE 10x42s that are smaller in size, lighter in weight, and are exceptionally bright and sharp. I field-tested a pair of 10x45 Zeiss Nite Owls that are incredible glasses when it comes to sharpness and light-gathering abilities. There are a number of excellent binoculars on the market, so take your time in choosing a pair and you'll be well rewarded for your efforts.

Serious scouting any time of the year also requires a good spotting scope and there are plenty to choose from. I much prefer a variable-power scope of 15X to 45X. I often use the scope on the lower setting to scope distant ridges and areas much as I utilize binoculars. If I locate a suspicious object or deer I zoom in on higher power to get a better look. The Swarovski T-80, 20-60X spotting scope is one of the best I have ever used and also one of the most expensive. For general spotting in all light conditions, where weight and size are not a factor, I use a 15-45X variable, power Nikon ED II Fieldscope. This ultra-sharp scope has the same quality low-light dispersion glass in its lenses as my superexpensive Nikon camera lenses. For really long-distance work, I also have a 60X eyepiece that replaces the variable eyepiece. Many a whitetail has been carefully looked over, judged, patterned, and recorded for posterity in my notes without ever having been the wiser due to this distance-cutting piece of glass. Where weight is a factor, such as scouting in the backcountry or from the top of a tree, I use a lightweight 16-47X variable power, rubber armored, waterproof, Nikon XL Spotter. Bushnell also makes an excellent line of spotting scopes that are reasonably priced and will more than fill the needs of most whitetail hunters. Redfield, Leupold, and Bausch & Lomb also produce superb spotting scopes. Go to a large sporting goods store and compare several scopes until you find one that will fill your needs within your budget.

A good spotting scope is useless without a solid base to hold it steady during your scouting outings. You can build a cheap serviceable scope rest out of a canvas bank money bag or 25# shot sack filled with kitty litter that will work fine across the hood of your vehicle or on a rock or log. A small, cheap, collapsible tripod available at any camera store is a lot easier to pack around and just as serviceable. Spotting from a vehicle calls for a solid window mount. One of the best, lightweight window mounts I have used is made by Bogen and can be bought through a camera store. Bogen also makes a camera mount called the Super Clamp with a swivel head that works great for holding a spotting scope in all sorts of situations. It can be clamped to just about anything and will squeeze the juice out of an oak limb. Don't try to use this clamp on a vehicle window because it can easily break the glass when cranked down.

A good notebook is another key piece of equipment that should be a constant companion on all your hunting and scouting trips. I am the world's worst when it comes to taking notes but over the past few years of dealing with whitetails, my notebooks and the information they contain have proved invaluable. There are several specially designed deer hunting logs on the market but I just settle for a spiral-bound pad that fits in my shirt pocket. Recording such things as deer sightings, buck sizes, weather and wind conditions at stand locations along with dates and time, location of major trails, funnels, travel corridors, signpost rubs and scrapes, and the hodgepodge of other information that pops up daily will often keep you from forgetting little details that could make the difference in your success or failure. When I get back from a scouting trip I'll transcribe the info from my notebook to my computer for future referencing and study in conjunction with my topo maps and aerial photos.

ELECTRONIC SCOUTING

In this age of high tech it's only natural that whitetail hunters would find a GPS or Global Positioning System unit useful in their scouting endeavors. This little hand-held outfit is a real marvel of modern technology that can be used to pinpoint any specific location in the world. GPS units are supposed to have a random offset that limits their accuracy to 100 meters, but in real-life use they are accurate to within 10 meters 90 percent of the time. This random offset factor was set by the government to keep their accuracy marginal for military reasons. This government restriction was removed this last summer and the newer civilian units on the market should have the capability of locating positions within feet and inches. GPS units can be put to good use in scouting to locate the position of such things as rub lines, scrapes, springs, saddles, major trails, funnels, individual food sources, and much more. Several of the GPS units on the market are no larger than a TV control unit and even the larger units will easily fit in a day pack or fanny pack.

These units are fairly simple to operate in the field. The first step would be to record your camp, home, or some other base of operations as a key waypoint. From this you could head into the field and add individual waypoints consisting of scrapes, funnels, saddle crossings, rub lines, bedding areas, feeding areas, etc. This information could then be accurately transferred to your U.S.G.S. maps to give you a better overall view of what's happening in your hunting area. Several units have the capability of "dumping" info directly into a computer for storage and retrieval when you need it. With this capability you could store data from different areas of the country or hunting camps and when you get ready to head for that area you could load the data into your GPS and the unit would lead you right to each previous waypoint with unbelievable ease.

One of the major deficiencies of some GPS units is their inability to acquire satellite lock-on through heavy over-head cover, which would stop you from getting a precise reading. In such a situation you may have to move to the nearest clearing for a reading and then figure in your own offset to get back to that scrape or white oak tree. A GPS unit might be a bit overwhelming or "over gunning" if you are only scouting a 40-acre tract of land behind the barn, but if you are hunting large timbered areas or vast tracts of private or public land and use it enough to realize its capa-bility for use under scouting situations, you'll never leave home without it. The days of getting lost or not being able to find a specific scrape or white oak tree in the swamp or forest are long gone with a GPS in your pack.

Unfortunately proper scouting takes much more time than many hunters are able to give, because of the fast-paced, time-consuming and ultra competitive work world they have to endure in order to keep the wolf away from the door and still be able to spend a few precious days in the whitetail woods.

Even those dedicated and fortunate individuals who spend day after day scouting on a year-round basis, trying to narrow the whitetail's chances of surviving to a mini-mum and their chances of success to a maximum, don't have the time or determination and perseverance to spend 24 hours a day during the two or three months of the sea-son observing whitetail activity.

Learning a whitetail's movement patterns or getting a

The Trailtimer Plus 500 is simple to use and will record up to 500 events.

passing deer's photo during the hours of darkness is often as important to a hunter as knowing their daytime movements. Gaining this info can be a difficult, if not impossible, task using conventional scouting methods but due to modern technology, all is not lost.

My first experience with trail timers or automatic trail monitoring devices of any sort was during bear season, when I tried to get a time frame on a trophy bear that wasn't following the script and coming to the bait during shooting hours. I used a simple little device called the Trailtimer. This contraption consisted of a small plastic case containing a digital clock, spool of thread, nylon string, and a little plastic loop. The clock was set to the correct time with the bottom of the loop shoved into a slot in the clock, depressing the on/off switch and keeping the clock running. The small unit was then tied to any solid object adjacent to the trail to be monitored. One end of the thread was tied to the bottom of the loop and the other to a solid object across the animal's route of travel. When the animal hit the thread, the tension before the thread broke, pulled the plastic loop out of the clock and stopped it at the exact time the animal passed. When the thread breaks, the broken ends are carried in the direction the animal was traveling. This simple, foolproof, pocket-size device gives the hunter both the time and direction of any passing critter. The Trailtimer is probably used by more deer hunters today than any other trail monitoring device because of its low price and its ease of use.

There are a number of good trail monitoring units on the market today and you should have no problem finding just the right one for your needs. However, not all of them are the same, nor do they accomplish the same purpose, so it's extremely important for you to decide just how you want to use a trail monitor and what information you need it to provide to increase your knowledge of deer movements. Let me tell you, right up front, that using an electronic trail monitoring device is darn sure not going to give you a lock on getting a trophy buck or let you take unfair advantage of any wary record-class buck. What trail monitors will do is allow you to increase your knowledge of deer movements and habits, in absentia, and provide you with more specific and accurate information on deer habits in your hunting area, and possibly a photo series of the deer using a specific trail, scrape, or feeding area, in a shorter time frame than would be otherwise possible.

There are two basic types of modern, high-tech, infrared trail monitoring devices on the market today. The active infrared monitors make use of two separate units. One is a transmitter that sends out a narrow, invisible beam across the trail, much like stretching out a ⅜" trip rope across the area to be monitored. The beam is targeted to hit the small sensor in the receiver. Anything that disrupts or breaks this beam will trigger the circuits in the receiver and the time, date, and event number will be recorded in the unit's memory. The monitor will also trigger a camera at the same time, if the unit is programmed for this function. The unit will store this information until you come along and get a readout. An active infrared beam is sensitive enough to record the passing of a hummingbird but is normally adjusted to a point where only a large animal such as a deer will trip it. This eliminates the chance of false readings given by the passing of smaller animals or birds. The active infrared's main advantages are its reliability when it comes to providing accurate information and its wide range of sensitivity. The main disadvantage is the need for two separate units; this means higher initial cost.

Most of the trail monitors on the market today are passive infrared units. Passive infrared monitors operate on a heat and motion principle, and only need a single unit to monitor an area. The passive infrared monitors throw a series of invisible infrared pulses at intervals across the area to be monitored. Any critter interrupting one or more of these pulses within a given amount of time with its body heat or motion will be registered as an individual event, trigger a camera, or do both depending on the type of unit.

Single-unit passive monitors are somewhat cheaper than the active units, and can be set up under a greater variety of situations. On the other hand they can be touchier to set up in the field because their broad field of view and method of operation can cause them to record moving, inanimate objects such as sun-warmed branches, cornstalks, weeds, etc., moving in the midday breeze as events, and give a false activity reading. Once you fully understand how these units work and what they can accomplish under actual field conditions, you shouldn't have any problem setting them up.

The most important step in getting the best "bang for your buck" is to decide just what information you want to obtain from a trail monitoring unit and then find the best outfit for the money that will accomplish your objective.

A weekend hunter might want to use one or more units on several deer trails or scrapes during the week to monitor the deer movements. On Friday evening the hunter can check the units to get the dates and times of the week's deer activity. He could study the activity patterns and make optimum use of his limited hunting time on Saturday and Sunday by hunting the trail or scrape that showed the most consistent use during legal hunting hours throughout the week.

Some hunters might want to get the same information and also have photos of the deer so he can get a look at their headgear. Another might just be interested in getting deer photos and not so much in getting the times and dates of the deer passing by.

As an outfitter with a new whitetail hunting operation in Iowa, I want to learn as much about the whitetail movements on our leases as efficiently and quickly as I can. Consequently, I use a number of the units, both active and passive, to monitor trails, scrapes, crossings, and rub lines, throughout the fall hunting season. I want to know when the deer are crossing between cornfields and the adjacent timber. What changes in their travel patterns occur with the harvesting of crops or the onset of the rut? What times do they leave a bedding area and return? What time do they arrive at a holding or loitering area? What increase or decrease in activity in certain areas occurs during the first gun season? When, during the season, are deer most active around waterholes? As the bow season progresses, do they change their patterns from daylight hours to darkness or vice versa? What type of weather conditions trigger heavy use of food plots?

To get as many answers as possible we set out trail monitors at the first of the season and gathered data intermittently throughout the whole season. Over the space of a couple of years of closely monitoring a number of key locations in our hunting area, we should gain some valuable insight into the activities of the local whitetail population. This knowledge should make us better at our craft and we might even be able to outsmart a trophy buck or two for our clients because of it.

I started using the Trailmaster monitors built by Goodson & Associates a number of years ago. At the time the only models available were the active infrared units. These units would store 1,000 events and run for about a month on a set of four C batteries for each of the transmitter and receiver units.

When a camera is attached to the unit you can program the Trailmaster to start taking photos at certain times and stop at specified times. Bill Goodson, the designer of the units, has since brought out a passive unit that will also take a camera hookup, and has specified starting and stopping times for the camera's operation. All Trailmaster units have full adjustment for the sensitivity of the pulses and the time frame in which they must be broken. Roughly, this means you can adjust the Trailmaster units to record critters as small as a hummingbird flying through the beam or react to nothing smaller than a slow-walking deer-size animal. All of the units are waterproof, and will operate at any temperature encountered in the field.

The Trailmaster series also has a plug-in for a small data printer so you can get a printed readout from your Trail-

CamTrakker will automatically photograph any deer passing through the infrared beam.

master unit right in the field by simply plugging in a connecting cord and touching a couple of buttons. Trailmaster also has a data collector unit and a computer program, which allows a hunter with several of these units out in the woods to carry the collector into the field, plug it into the trail monitor, push a couple of buttons, and dump the data from the monitor into the collector, all in the blink of an eye. You can gather data from as many as 16 different monitors and then transfer this data to your computer at home. You can then merge it with previous data from the same location and get a printout of the data in graph or printed form. With the Trailmaster units it's possible to store a whole season's data in your computer to be studied at your leisure. These units are for the serious deer hunter and will add a whole new dimension to your learning about whitetail habits and idiosyncrasies and keeping records of the same for future use and interpretation.

Trailtimer, the manufacturers of the little string monitor mentioned earlier, offers an easy mounting, passive unit that will record and store 500 events and operates on one nine-volt battery. This unit has a small focused circular beam, three feet in diameter at 60 feet. This configuration helps to eliminate false signals and faulty data. The unit does not have a camera hook-up. However, this unit is compatible with Trailtimer's TT 2000 camera system. They also lack printer ports and data dump capabilities but these units should fit the budget of most whitetail hunters.

The Deerfinder Game Monitor, manufactured by Non-Typical Engineering, is a unique piece of equipment in many ways. The monitor itself is a rugged, compact, black ABS plastic unit measuring 2 by 6½ inches. Its main weight comes from the single D-cell battery used to power the unit for up to four months. The unit will record up to 500

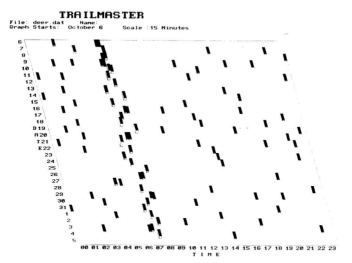

TRAILMASTER graph showing deer travel times past monitor. Ideal time to hunt location would be between 6 and 8 a.m.

events and can also be used in conjunction with a camera to get a photo of the critter tripping the monitor. Similar to other passive monitors, the Deerfinder uses a cone-shaped beam that will detect an animal's body heat out to approximately 60 feet under ideal conditions.

The similarity stops when you pick up the hand calculator–sized keyboard that accompanies the Deerfinder monitor. This little keyboard is the brains of the outfit and turns the detector unit on and off, sets it in either Deerfinder mode, where it simply monitors and records deer movements, or in DeerCam mode, where it records events and trips the connected camera. This little unit also is distinctive in that the detector unit can be protected by a password so that only you can turn it on or off. This feature was designed to discourage someone from stealing the monitor for use with their keyboard. Neat touch. The Deerfinder unit also has an adjustable event delay control, which means you can adjust the time after an event is recorded before it will record another event. This precludes getting a hundred event recordings of a buck making a scrape. Most preset units operate on a one event per minute basis but with this unit you can vary the time from 1 to 99 seconds or from 1 to 99 minutes. The Deerfinder also allows the user to program in a certain time frame that the camera can be activated. It can also be programmed to operate 24 hours a day. The user can also control the camera delay sequence, the same as with the event delay sequence, and program the camera activity to take a single photo or two photos two seconds apart.

When recording events, the Deerfinder will record up to 500 events and then continue to record the most recent event and delete the first (oldest) event, thereby giving you access to the most up-to-date event. With the keyboard unit you can read through the events by using up and down scrolling keys or you can use the auto recall button to bring the event up on the screen for a couple of seconds and then it will scroll on to the next event. At present there is no way to save the events other than to write down the data by hand, but company personnel told me that it would be very possible in the future to provide a data dump unit, along with a computer program, to store information provided by the detectors.

Many hunters are strictly interested in getting photos of the deer they have been hunting all season and for them the CamTrakker may be just the ticket. This unit consists of a passive infrared sensor unit connected to an autofocus, autowind, autoflash 35mm camera—all housed in a waterproof ABS plastic housing. The whole unit fastens to a tree, post, or other solid object overlooking a trail, scrape, or feeder and you simply set the unit to operate the camera

With a CamTrakker monitor it is possible to build up a photo album of *deer that passed your stand when you weren't around. You may see bucks you've never seen in daylight.*

continuously, day only or night only, set the delay between photos to one of the three options, either three, six, or 10 minutes and you are in business. The camera has a date-and-time feature so when you get the photos back from the processor you will know when the photo was taken. This unit is a simple and relatively foolproof way to get photos of the critters you are chasing around the woods.

Most of these trail monitoring units operate in much the same way and things that create a problem for one unit will probably create a problem for others as well. Over several years of utilizing these devices, I have probably made every mistake known to man and come up with several that were entirely new. Practice with the monitors in the off-season so you are completely familiar with their operation and the little things that can give you false information.

Some of the things I have learned from past experience:

1. Always fasten the monitors to solid objects. A moving base will often cause the unit to trigger and give you a mass of false readings.
2. Keep the units in the shadows and out of direct sunlight to avoid false readings.
3. Make sure there are no major movable objects in the unit's field of view that can change temperature as the day warms up and move in the breeze to give false readings.
4. Keep the units level so you get maximum and equal coverage of the activity zone.
5. If you're using a camera with your monitor make sure the unit and the camera are compatible. Some of the newer cameras go into a "sleep" mode after not being activated for a time and the unit's circuitry may not be capable of turning the camera back on.

Electronic trail monitors aren't going to guarantee you a shot at a big buck but they can broaden your knowledge of deer activity and habits. Knowledge is often your best defense against getting "whupped" repeatedly by those antlered, demon whitetails, and your best weapon for adding a trophy whitetail rack to your collection.

CHAPTER FOUR

SCOUTING THE WIND

"Blessed are those that hunt in a steady wind for they shall be the most successful!"

There should be no doubt in any serious whitetail hunter's mind about the importance WIND plays in their success or failure. Wind, and its propensity for carrying the dreaded human scent to the super-sensitive nostrils of a wary whitetail, is probably responsible for more than 90 percent of the unsuccessful encounters between hunter and deer. Even though many hunters are aware of this important aspect of their whitetail hunting ventures, most don't fully understand the idiosyncrasies of the wind and air currents that can wreak havoc with their chances, don't know how to use the wind to their advantage, or simply don't give a damn and go on their way in ignorant bliss.

Many hunters are vaguely aware of wind patterns in hilly country where the wind rises as the sun comes up and falls down the slope as the sun sets. If only dealing with wind currents were that simple we would all be a lot more successful. Add a few gulleys on the slope, thickets of trees, rock ledges, or open parks and you have wind patterns, currents, updrafts, downdrafts, swirls, and counter currents that can drive you nuts and defeat even the best-laid hunting plans. Ever wonder why deer and especially mature bucks like to travel below the ridges and above the bottoms of the draws? Obviously the visibility is better and they are not being skylined on the top of the ridge, but the main reason to my way of thinking is the simple fact that the wind currents on the sides of the slopes are far more stable and predictable and the deer can use them with much more confidence to detect danger from above or below depending on their flow. The breezes on the top of a ridge and in the valley or gully bottoms are as unpredictable and thereby as undependable for the deer as they are for the hunters, so the deer travel where they can depend on stable air currents.

In flat country, wind currents are much more predictable but can still give you fits unless you take some time to study their patterns and learn all you can about their idiosyncrasies as they apply to your particular hunting area. Such terrain features as dark-colored plowed or lush green fields that absorb more heat during the day than the surrounding woods can cause updrafts of warm air as the evening cools. This could mean that a hunter in a treestand at the edge of the field would be undetectable to any deer along the edge or in the field while a hunter 100 yards back in the woods may have his scent swirling down around his stand and spooking every deer within a 50-yard radius. A steady breeze, hitting a brushy stream bank or other natural obstacle in its path may be deflected high enough in the air on the far side of the obstacle to carry a hunter's scent far above the nose of any approaching whitetail, provided you stay within the area affected by the updraft. A lot can be learned about air movement when it encounters obstacles by taking the time to study water currents in a stream full of logs or rocks. Most of the time you can gain a decided advantage by knowing just how wind currents operate and by studying them in your hunting area.

I would rather put my faith in the wind and make it work for me rather than against me. If you have the wind currents, drafts, breezes, thermals, or whatever you want to call them

The only way you are going to fool a mature buck is to keep your scent away from his keen nose.

working in your favor you are going to win more encounters than you lose. There are always going to be occasions when Mother Nature throws you a split-second downdraft, up-draft, or thermal swirl that will ruin your day but heck, the deer have to win a few.

The most valuable hunting tool I have found for winning

Use of a squeeze bottle filled with talcum powder will let you check wind direction around your treestand.

Stand placement should be totally dependent on wind direction if you are going to be successful.

the war of winds is a simple but effective squeeze bottle full of talcum powder. Many whitetail hunters tie a piece of dental floss or feather to their bow or gun and use it to determine wind currents. This is far better than simply ignoring the wind as most unsuccessful deer hunters do, but a feather or floss falls far short of being as effective a wind indicator as a powder bottle.

There is always air movement!! With a powder bottle you can pick up the most subtle breeze, updraft, downdraft, or almost undetectable convection current or thermal drift. Constant use of a powder bottle during your scouting trips, while you are walking through your hunting area, or sitting in a treestand will continually upgrade your knowledge of the wind characteristics in your hunting area and go a long way toward letting you avoid detection by a wary buck's sense of smell. Noting the weather and wind conditions in your hunting area and around your stands during various times of the year, in your scouting notebook will give you a ready reference for future use and may be your most important entries.

Being constantly aware of wind currents is more important to bowhunters than gun hunters simply because of the "up-close-and-personal," distances involved. However, a gun hunter that doesn't pay attention to the wind is missing a sure step in becoming a better and more successful hunter. A bowhunter must avoid the deer's keen sense of smell at point-blank range where there is no distance factor to dilute or disperse the dreaded human scent. Any whitetail catching the slightest whiff of human scent at 30 yards or less is history for the waiting bowhunter. If the deer is a mature buck you can probably write that stand or particular area off for the rest of the season as far as that specific deer is concerned.

Many bowhunters take all the precautions in the book to kill or cover their odor. They shower, shave, and wash their hair and clothes in scent-eliminating soaps and solutions. They spray and splash all sorts of concoctions on themselves and anything else that will hold still, to eliminate or cover the human odor—all in hopes they can fool a deer's nose into thinking they don't exist. These precautions are all fine and good, when combined with scent-free, clean, outer clothing and footgear, and taking measures to leave as little scent on trails, bushes, fences, trees, and such in your hunting area and near a stand location. All this preparation might dilute the human scent enough to allow a deer to pass through the area without reaching the panic stage and help in allowing what scent there is to dissipate more rapidly. I don't personally feel there is anything on the market at this

A buck's nose can pick up the slightest trace of human scent on the ground.

point that will keep a hunter completely scent free, under most hunting conditions.

The best way to make these precautions work for your benefit most of the time is to make the wind work for you all the time! A powder bottle is the tool that can make this possible. You can use a powder bottle to check the wind from a number of different locations around a proposed stand location to determine a site where the wind is the least likely to betray your presence. There are times when simply moving your treestand a few trees one way or the other or placing your stand a few feet higher in the tree will get you into an entirely different wind current flow and totally eliminate the chances of a deer smelling you. Studying the drift of the talcum powder will often easily pinpoint such a location for you. You may have located a super deer funnel that can be hunted all day if it wasn't for the wind changing. By interpreting the wind drift at the different times of day with your powder bottle you can erect several stands to cover the area regardless of the wind conditions. When you are actually hunting such an area, use your powder bottle periodically to check the wind. If the wind switches unexpectedly the powder will tell you and it's a simple matter to climb down and carefully move to one of the other stands. Much better than being detected and blowing the whole setup.

Under hunting conditions a drifting cloud of talcum may just alert you to a wind change that could make a difference in where you take a shot. Several years ago I was bowhunting in Alberta, Canada, with an outfitter and not having much success. His wife had been scouting a winter wheat field one evening and spotted two P&Y bucks and several does feeding in a small pocket adjacent to a section of heavy bush. The next morning while I was hunting another area the outfitter and his wife returned to the field to put in a stand for me. Since there were no trees along the edge of the

Ron Wadsworth with a nice buck taken by keeping the wind in his favor during a stalk.

field that would hold a treestand, they improvised and dug and brushed up a shallow pit blind for me. That afternoon, his wife dropped me at the blind and I settled down for the wait. The afternoon was hot and the stiff breeze was quartering across my front, eliminating any chance of deer winding me approaching the field on the well-used trail in the corner

Applying deer scent or scent eliminator to your boots may confuse deer and keep them from panicking.

Rubber-bottom boots will have less tendency to leave human scent on the ground.

of the pocket. As the evening progressed the clouds bunched up over me and let loose with a torrential downpour for fifteen minutes. As the sun lowered and the air cooled, the breeze died, but the talcum from my trusty powder bottle told me that there was an almost imperceptible current of air drifting directly across the field in front of me. No problem!

As the evening progressed and the sun settled behind a cloud bank, several does moved out of the brush into the field and began feeding voraciously on the lush green wheat. Now I had a problem! One of the does was feeding my way about 10 yards from the edge of the brush line. If she got opposite me there was little doubt that she was going to be inundated by my cloud of scent drifting slowly across the field. To make matters worse, two fine bucks, both in the 140-plus category, emerged from the corner of the bush and began feeding on an angle toward me. I eased my bow into shooting position and again tested the wind with a thin stream of talc. The current was holding steady as I watched the doe and bucks moving closer. The doe was now less than 15 yards from me while the bucks were still 45 yards out. Fortunately the doe found an extra-special clump of sedge to munch for a few extra seconds and gave the bucks a chance to cut the distance to 40 yards. When the doe started moving again I tensed for the shot. She was less than 10 yards from my blind and probably only five yards from the edge of my scent stream when I centered my concentration on the larger buck, drew, and released. He had been a bit farther than I preferred but the arrow was right on and he was down for the count within 100 yards. At my shot the doe exploded into action and headed back into the brush. If I hadn't been using a powder bottle there was a very good chance that I would have unknowingly let the doe move into my scent stream and blow the whole show, as I waited for the bucks to move within 25 yards or less. My trusty, tell-all, powder bot-

Judd Cooney testing the wind with his ever-present powder bottle.

tle has saved the day for me on a number of similar occasions with whitetails, elk, antelope, and bear.

A cloud of talc can also let you know when your chances of success in hunting a certain stand are zero and you had better call it quits before you ruin a good stand. Last fall I was bowhunting from a morning stand that overlooked a major trail leading to a couple of food plots. The early morn-

A cloud of powder is a foolproof indicator of the slightest wind current.

ing weather was cool with heavily overcast skies and the likelihood of rain. The subtle breeze drifting through the woods, in my favor, made detection by any deer approaching from the food plot or the timbered slopes unlikely. Just as it was getting light enough to shoot the skies opened up in a cold shower that cooled everything down considerably. I had anticipated a wet hunt and had on my rain gear and the treestand umbrella in place. I figured with a cool, damp morning and the rut in progress there was a good chance deer would be moving all morning and a good buck might just check the area around the food plot for scent of a doe in estrus. Five minutes after the shower, the breeze died completely—well, almost! The cloud of talcum emitted from my plastic bottle settled around the base of the tree under my stand like an ever-expanding mushroom. I had no doubt the longer I stayed put the larger the cloud of scent would become, and envelope the whole section of woods, just hanging there to alert any and all approaching deer to my presence. The odds of ruining this stand for future hunting were far better than the chances of my getting a shot at a good buck so I simply packed up and eased out of the area to wait for a morning when the air currents were in my favor.

A powder bottle is a deadly accessory for still-hunting and stalking also. There are times when you can stalk a deer or likely bedding area from the upwind side *If* you know exactly what the wind and air currents are doing. Oftentimes, all you have to do to keep your scent out of a likely place to jump a buck is to move slightly off to one side, just enough to let your scent be carried past the patch of cover and not into it. By periodically monitoring the wind with your powder bottle you can almost always hunt with the breeze in your favor and greatly increase your chances of success.

I carry squeeze bottles of talcum in all my fanny and day packs, camera bag, bow and gun kits, glove compartments of my vehicles, and even one in my shaving kit, just in case. There are a lot of things I might leave behind when I go scouting or hunting but you can bet your bippy one of them isn't going to be my windicator powder bottle.

CHAPTER FIVE

SPRINGTIME SCOUTING

Spring, the time when a hen turkey's thoughts turn to what the gobblers have been thinking about all winter, is also the time when a serious whitetail hunter's thoughts should be turning toward the coming fall hunting season.

The visions of the past deer hunting season are still fresh enough to create a vivid picture in your mind of the big bucks you saw and never got, the bucks that just didn't quite get within bow range while it was still light enough for a good shot, and the bucks you saw during the season in areas where you had least expected them to appear.

This past fall I spent two months in Iowa, guiding whitetail gun and bowhunters after some of the most awesome bucks to leave a track in the dirt. My partners Ruby Custer, son-in-law Mike Kraetsch, and I started Iowa Trophy Whitetail Outfitters with the idea of providing a top-class hunt for a limited number of shotgun, muzzleloader, and bowhunters in some of the finest big buck country in North America.

The last week in October Bill Jordan, president of Realtree Inc., an addicted trophy buck hunter, brought M. R. James, editor of *Bowhunter Magazine* and Gregg Miller, well-known whitetail author and seminar lecturer, along with him to give our operation a try.

One of our leased hunting properties, not far from hunting camp, consisted of approximately 160 acres of an open bowl–shaped valley of Conservation Reserve Program land, grown up in knee-high grass and weeds, surrounded on three sides by heavy, hardwood timber. On the upper north side, the CRP valley was a high, hardwood ridge bordering a huge tract of rugged, gully-seamed, timbered country, where no hunting was allowed. A "big buck" sanctuary for sure! The south and western edges of the property were also bordered by high grassy ridges interspersed with timber and cedars. There was a finger of sparse timber and cedar extending from the southern boundary into the meadow, just opposite a wider finger extending from the northwestern corner. The area certainly wasn't very imposing looking and not exactly the kind of area you would expect to be a "big buck" hot spot.

Just prior to Bill's arrival we had seen a good buck in the area and set up a couple of stands on trails leading into the CRP from the sanctuary to the north. Several days of windy weather kept deer movement to a minimum but a cold snap put the big bucks in the mood and got them up and moving. During the next few days, Gregg missed a monstrous buck that would have scored in the high 190's and arrowed another that made Pope & Young. A few days later, a squeaky treestand cost Bill Jordan a shot at another buck that would have scored over 170. Not bad for an area that we hadn't taken nearly enough time to scout out thoroughly prior to hunting season. By the end of the season we had located several other good trails where we could probably have ambushed a buck when they were really on the move.

It wasn't until this spring, during a combination spring turkey hunt and scouting trip, that I really learned about the deer movements in that particular area. The adjacent farm to the south is also one of our leases but we had agreed not to hunt that piece of the property. It was behind

Judd Cooney, Mike Waddell, and Chris Kirby with two turkeys and antler sheds. Combining spring scouting with turkey hunting is a great way to learn more about whitetails.

the farmer's home and his wife liked to watch the turkeys and deer in the bean fields around the house.

This spring I spent considerable time photographing the turkeys that used a couple of large oaks in the center of the cedar thicket as a roost and the open meadows as strutting areas. By covering a considerable amount of country in and around both pieces of property scouting for trails, rubs, scrapes, and beds while I was turkey hunting, photographing, and looking for sheds I learned a hell of a lot about the travel patterns of the deer living in and around that area. I located several deer trails leading from the CRP along the timbered ridges and draws to the bedding area. These trails had innumerable rubs along their course. I found another well-used trail just inside the brush and timber along the finger ridge bordering the broad expanse of open CRP. This cedar-, brush-, and timber-covered ridge is a natural travel corridor for the bucks moving between the doe holding and bedding area of impenetrable cedars and fields of corn and beans to the south and the heavy timbered sanctuary area to the north. The bucks threading their way along this side-hilling trail would be able to visually check much of the open CRP area below the ridge for does and still stay under cover provided by the brush and trees. A deer only had 150 yards of open CRP to cross after leaving the dense oakbrush thicket at the lower end of the point, before it was protected once again by the heavy timber. A natural funnel for ambushing a buck on the move during the rut. You can bet that early next fall we'll be sneaking treestands into these key areas where the bucks least expect them. Just maybe we'll be able to get a client in the right place at the right time and give him a chance at one of those humongous bucks that should be even larger this coming fall.

Many early season rubs and rub lines can be scouted out by a careful hunter during the initial part of the pre-rut without doing irreparable damage and alerting every buck in the area of your presence. A savvy hunter that is deadly serious about big buck hunting is wise to be overly cautious about scouting every nook and cranny and following rub lines into the middle of a trophy buck's core area and bedding ground. Taking a chance on leaving the slightest hint of human presence and blowing a chance at a big buck might not be a wise decision. Especially when you can do a more thorough and much lower impact job of scouting rub and scrape lines and get the same information without doing any serious deer spooking.

Spring turkey hunting and spring scouting for whitetails is a natural combination because turkeys and deer are both

Spring burning can reveal trails used during fall and winter and pin-point stand locations for the coming fall.

creatures of habit and cover much the same country. This seems to hold true whether you are hunting Merriam's turkeys in the Dakotas or Montana, Eastern gobblers in Iowa or Alabama, or Rio Grande gobblers in Texas or Oklahoma. Usually where you find turkeys you find deer. Having a valid turkey license in your pocket and carrying a bow or shotgun on your spring scouting trips can give you a powerful incentive to spend long hours traipsing around the woods keeping your eyes and ears open. Often chasing a gobbling turkey will lead you into places you probably wouldn't have gotten to in your normal scouting and deer hunting forays. A spring turkey is an opportunist with an intimate knowledge of his home range and may lead you to hidden feeding areas in deep woods that you didn't know existed; an area that would make an excellent place to find and ambush a deer during the fall hunting season.

Following an old gobbler working the ridgetops looking for hens is also a good way to locate a deer crossing or trail

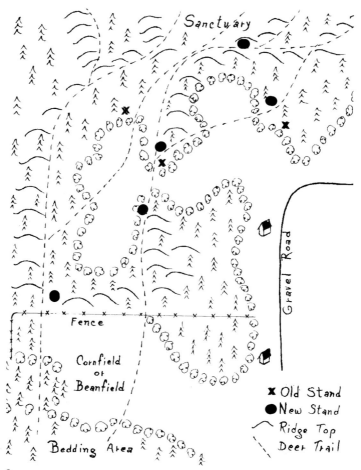

Sanctuary

Gravel Road

Fence

Cornfield
or
Beanfield

Bedding Area

x Old Stand
● New Stand
⌒ Ridge Top
╲ Deer Trail

Spring scouting an area that had been hot during the fall, I found several new stand locations.

that you didn't know existed or one that maybe didn't exist the last time you were in the area.

Several springs back I was turkey hunting with a good friend on his farm and keeping my eyes open for past

Not all deer will make it through the winter. Along with sheds you'll find the remains of some bucks that won't be there next fall.

whitetail activity when a gobbler started sounding off from the top of an adjacent ridgetop. It didn't take long for us to figure he was with a bunch of hens and we needed to change locations and give the hens time to leave before working him again. We decided to cut across a deep flat-bottomed draw where he had placed a treestand overlooking a well-used deer trail. He had seen a number of does and small bucks from the stand the previous fall but the big bucks had eluded him, even though he knew there were several in the area. We followed an old fenceline up the steep sidehill and about fifty yards below the top of the ridge we found where a strand of the barbed wire fence had been broken by a falling limb sometime during the previous fall. The deer had evidently found the break and the easy crossing and had changed their pattern of travel to make use of the downed fence. During the early fall my friend put a treestand overlooking the fence crossing and arrowed a beautiful 10-point 150-class buck the second evening in the stand, after passing up several smaller bucks.

The bucks much preferred staying in the heavier timber along the sidehill rather than using the top of the ridge or the valley bottom, a trait common to most older mature bucks. I figure they like to travel on the sidehills for much the same reasons I do or vice versa. A buck traveling along the side of the ridge is not skylined or in the bright sunshine and can easily see the slightest movement on the ridgetop above him, be it a two- or four-legged predator, turkey, or another deer. A buck is much more liable to travel on the shady side of the ridge during midday than the sunny side as he can see danger much easier in the less contrasting light and is in a better position on the sidehill to spot danger from below. Normally the wind currents are much steadier and dependable, whether rising or falling,

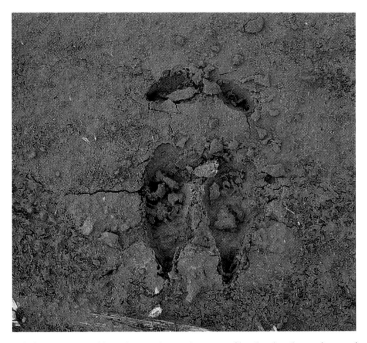

While it's impossible to know the antler size of bucks that have dropped their racks, presence of very large tracks is always a good indication of mature, trophy bucks.

along the slope of the hill than they are on the top of the ridge or at the bottom of a draw where they have a decided tendency to dip and swirl. A mature buck is darn sure going to travel where he can trust the wind.

The downed fence funneled most of the bucks to that one crossing. A little change in a deer's surrounding can often make drastic changes in their habits and patterns. Keeping our eyes open and scouting with whitetails in mind during our spring turkey outing put my buddy in position to take the biggest buck of his career. It also made

A prominent signpost rub like this is quite noticeable, even months after the season—and it will be worth investigating in the fall!

a firm believer out of him when it comes to the value of spring scouting.

SHED-ANTLER HUNTING AND SCOUTING

Shed-antler hunting is another way to add interest to your spring scouting ventures and can also provide you with valuable information on the size and quality of the bucks running around in your hunting area. Shed hunting is a fast-growing springtime endeavor with its own organization, North American Shed Hunters Club Inc. This record-keeping group has published a book, *Shed Antler Records of North American Big Game.* A number of organizations in some of the midwestern states have shed-antler contests each spring with some pretty hefty prizes; and from what I hear the competition is pretty stiff.

Shed antlers are easier to locate early in the spring before the vegetation can grow over them and the squirrels, porcupines, and other rodents utilize them as a source of concentrated calcium. Finding shed antlers in your hunting area will tell you quickly the age and size of the bucks that survived the hunting season and should still be around to challenge your hunting abilities during the next season. It may also give you a general idea of the area the real boomer bucks cover, at least during the late season. Shed antlers can often be found in tracts of heavy, brushy cover, low-lying areas, creek bottoms, plum and cedar thickets, or sloughs where bucks can escape the nasty weather during the late winter season. Finding antlers in such locations should give you a good reason to check the same areas (carefully) during the rut or in late season when hunting pressure might just push a buck into returning to such an undisturbed location. Near food plots or fields and along the trails and rub lines leading from the bedding areas to the feeding areas is also another good place to locate shed antlers.

If you have a really big buck located after the season and can keep fairly close track of his whereabouts during January and early February you can often find his sheds within a mile of your last sighting in areas of heavy cover where he is likely bedding or along well-used trails to feeding areas.

In states where baiting is legal, the area surrounding bait piles or feed stations is a good place to look for shed antlers but you had better be on the ball and get to these areas as soon as the snow gets off the ground and you can get to the locations. Shed-antler hunting is growing in popularity so rapidly that antler hunters are hitting these known locations with a vengeance.

There has been much talk about how baiting makes it too easy to take a big buck but in talking with a number of hunters in areas where baiting is allowed, this may not be the case nearly as much as people think. A number of hunters, guides, and outfitters using bait stations have told me that after the season, when they finished hunting for sheds around their bait stations, they were often astounded by the results. They found shed antlers from a number of huge bucks that they never once laid eyes on during the entire season. There is no doubt in my mind that a major portion of the older trophy bucks using a bait pile or feeder will never come to the bait or feed during the daylight hours, even during the peak of the rut. If they do come into the area in search of a hot doe, they are going to check the feeder from a safe distance downwind.

It's a frustrating and humbling experience to scout an area during the spring that you hunted during the entire fall bow and gun season and come away with four or five different shed antlers that will score in the 140 to 160 range while you or your fellow hunters never saw a single buck in that size category. It's also a darn good learning experience and will make you concentrate just that much more on using every scouting technique within your power to find those few special locations that will put you or your friends in the same place as one of those bucks at the same time the buck is there.

Spring is also a good time to thoroughly scout out suspected and known bedding areas that you located during

Shed hunting is an enjoyable spring pastime; the sheds are interesting "trophies" and where you find them is valuable information.

John Barhal found these sheds near his hunting area. This is one huge buck that made it through the winter, a good reason for a big smile.

the fall hunting season but didn't want to disturb because of the high likelihood of spooking a perceptive trophy-size buck completely out of the area. Easing quietly around and through a bedding area during your spring scouting is unlikely to have any long-lasting effect on any bucks you jump or that may pick up your scent in their hidey-hole. Fully scouting out these major bedding areas and sanctuaries will allow you to locate trails leading to and from the area. Checking the location of rubs on the trees in conjunction with these trails, and back-trailing them out of the area, should allow you to make an educated guess as to which trails are more likely to be used as exit trails for evening hunting and which are used as entrance trails for morning hunting. Scout out stand locations where you can take advantage of the buck's direction of travel and keep the wind in your favor, as well as choosing approach lanes to the stand locations that will minimize the chances of a buck crossing your trail and possibly getting a whiff of your scent.

In some cases, by back-trailing from a bedding area toward a feeding area, you can locate what I call a loafing or loitering area. Bucks moving from the bedding or sanctuary area, especially during the pre-rut, will often mill around or hold up in heavy cover near a feeding area until just before dark. These holding areas often have a number of seemingly random scrapes or rubs scattered over a relatively large yard area. Locating one or more of these holding areas during your spring scouting is like having money in the bank when the season gets near enough to start putting stands into position for the coming hunt. During the spring season you can cover your hunting area thoroughly without worrying about your scent driving a skittish old buck out of the country or making him change his pattern.

Make sure you keep detailed notes on all your scouting trips and file them in a place where they can be easily retrieved when the fall hunting season approaches. Aerial photos and U.S.G.S. maps with notes or icons penciled on them showing rub lines, scrapes, and bedding areas will make your fall preparations much easier and more efficient and that's going to increase your chances of scoring on one of those elusive trophy bucks.

Spring scouting is the nearest thing to fall hunting itself, without the pressure and urgency. When you throw in a good measure of shed-antler hunting and combine it with spring turkey hunting, you're probably going to be looking forward to the coming of spring scouting season almost as much as you do the fall hunting season.

CHAPTER SIX

SUMMER SCOUTING

As far as I'm concerned summer is the pits! It's hot, buggy, muggy, and there aren't any hunting seasons open. If it wasn't for the fact that whitetail fawns need a warm period with unlimited food supply to grow into bucks, while does need the same to produce possible record book bucks, and the trophy bucks themselves need the summer months to nourish and grow their massive antlers, I would vote to ban summer in favor of another three months of fall.

Scouting and observing deer during the hot, humid, summer evenings, and the somewhat cooler mornings, fortunately is not a total waste of time and far better than staying home and working on the roof or hoeing weeds in the garden.

During the summer months, whitetails limit their daily activities to eating, drinking, and sleeping. If you see deer movement, they are either on their way to a feeding or watering area, drinking or feeding, on their way to a bedding area, or bedded. Quite naturally they are going to be bedding in the protection and shade of the thickest, coolest, cover they can find and observing them there is next to impossible and wouldn't accomplish anything anyhow.

Cruising the countryside early in the morning and again at dusk and glassing alfalfa, clover, bean, oats, or cornfields should let you get a look at the deer that made it through

Deer are often not very visible during the hot summer, doing most feeding and moving during the cooler hours of darkness. Don't worry unduly if you see only the occasional white tail flagging.

the previous hunting season and winter. Make sure you update your notebook with the information.

One of the very best places to observe the deer during the summer months is on a waterhole. During hot weather deer will usually water at least twice a day and often will water during the middle of the day. This allows a patient observer a good look at the quality and number of deer using that particular area. For many Texas biologists and ranch managers, observing waterholes during the heat of the summer is the favorite method of censusing their deer numbers and also determining the size and quality of the bucks that have made it through hunting season and the winter months. By locating and checking ponds, streams, and tank dams for tracks and sign you can determine the amount of activity taking place and even get some idea of the size of the deer using the watering hole.

Toward midsummer, in most areas, you'll start to get a good idea of what a buck will look like when his antlers are fully formed.

Summer is the first time you can really have a good idea what sort of fawn crop and carryover your hunting area has to offer.

A few years back when I hunted in Alberta I asked my outfitter if he ever hunted waterholes for bucks or glassed them during the heat of summer to see what kind of bucks were using the area. He admitted that he hadn't paid them much attention as he assumed that the bucks would only use them at night. The thought had never occurred to him that this might be an excellent way to census deer and locate good bucks. The fact that there were no suitable trees for treestands near most of them also kept him from giving them more than a passing thought. During a midday lull we checked several waterholes located a couple of hundred

In the warmer months you may find deer concentrated in shady glades—and for sure you'll find them reasonably close to water.

yards from the edge of some dense bush country, ideal Alberta whitetail habitat. As I had suspected the waterhole was "covered up" with deer tracks. The location was perfect and when I showed the outfitter how to locate, dig, and camouflage a pit blind, one of the most deadly and efficient techniques of hunting open-country whitetails I have found. I created a whole new way of whitetail scouting and hunting for him. Since that time this Alberta outfitter's clients have taken some of their best early season bucks hunting from pit blinds overlooking waterholes.

There are many areas of the U.S. and Canada where the weather during the opening of archery season is still hot and dry and this makes waterholes a prime location for your stand. Scouting waterholes during the late summer will give you a good idea which waterholes have the best bucks using them and the best location for a stand to ambush the buck. You will probably find that the best time to hunt a hot weather waterhole is from midday until dark, which is a bit different from your normal early morning hunting.

You can't put yourself in this picture in the summer, but by considering scouting a year-round pastime your chances will be much improved when the actual hunting season arrives.

During the late summer months there might be some locations where you can put up an observation treestand on a ridge or other high point overlooking much of your hunting country. From this treestand you can scout and

Waterholes are a key location to census deer in hot summer months and to hunt for big bucks during early fall season.

observe deer movements and activity without taking a chance on spooking them. The more time you spend in your observation stand during the late summer months the more you will learn about the daily movements and patterns of your hunting season adversaries and the better prepared you will be for the opening of hunting season.

Digging a pit blind on an early season waterhole might produce big time.

Summer scouting is the best time of year to locate the home range of a real "boomer" buck or two and start trying to figure out where he will be when the season opens. Keep in mind, however, that some deer will change their areas of activity considerably from their summer areas to those where they will be during the fall hunting season. When the bucks begin to break up their bachelor groups, some, and especially the more dominant bucks, may move several miles from their summer feeding, watering, bedding, and friendly fraternizing areas to their fall core areas in preparation for the coming rut. If the lay of the land is such that you feel the trophy buck might just stay in the same general vicinity where you observed his activity during the summer months, you should start work on obtaining permission to hunt that section of country for the coming fall hunting season.

I have found it's much easier to get permission far in advance of the season than it is to wait until the day before you want to hunt and then try to locate the landowner and get permission. During the summer and early autumn a landowner is usually not as busy as they will be later in the season near harvesttime. At that time of year most landowners, farmers, or ranchers probably haven't been as inundated with requests for hunting permission as is likely to happen as the season draws near, a time when hunters are trying to pressure him for permission—right now! In such a preseason situation good P.R. (public relations) goes a long way. Inviting a landowner and his family out for dinner to get acquainted might be the best investment you can make. It just might also result in obtaining hunting permission or getting a lease to hunt the land for some time to come. Try to think of how you would like to be treated if the situation were reversed and you were the landowner, and act accordingly.

Summer scouting a good waterhole may locate the perfect spot for an early season pit blind.

Summer scouting may be a hot, buggy proposition but it just might put you onto a good buck using a hidden waterhole or let you pattern his movements sufficiently to be in the right place at the right time during the opening days of the fall season and end your hunt before it gets started.

CHAPTER SEVEN

SCOUTING THE
PRE-RUT AND RUT

As summer turns into fall and the days start getting shorter and cooler, things start happening in the world of the whitetail deer. As the buck's testosterone level starts to rise and their fully formed velvet-covered antlers harden, their demeanor also changes. The older and larger bucks begin to show signs of wanting to dominate the smaller bucks and all bucks start getting more aggressive toward one another. Around the last week in August and the first week of September, in most regions of the U.S. and Canada, the bucks shed their velvet and the pre-rut begins. Whitetail bucks completely shed the velvet from the antlers in a matter of hours. I once photographed a buck in full velvet at daylight one morning and at noon I photographed the same buck completely rubbed out and white antlered. The more mature bucks start to wander away from their bachelor buddies to explore and reacquaint themselves with their core areas and sanctuaries, where their prime concern, until the rut fully kicks in are food, security, and comfort.

The first rubs and scrapes begin to appear around the edges of feeding areas and fields and along the trails leading from bedding grounds to the food sources. One of the key areas to start your pre-rut scouting is around good food and water sources. During this period of the pre-rut

Early in the fall bucks are often concentrated in bachelor groups.

bucks are not going to be wandering around the countryside much and will usually be moving directly from their
bedding areas to food and water and then returning to the
bedding area or sanctuary. Along the way they will be exer-
cising their neck muscles and shoulders by thrashing the
local bushes and trees and creating very visual signs of
their passing. This can, indeed, be the toughest time of the
year to kill a really monster buck because of the limited
amount of time he is accessible and on the move in his
small core area. It can also be the easiest time to kill a mature buck, because he is usually traveling alone, hasn't
been pressured yet, and has fairly predictable travel and activity patterns. Good pre-hunt scouting is the major factor
determining whether this time of the season will be feast or
famine for the hunter.

Since the pre-rut activity generally takes place when
there is an early fall hunting season, especially if you are a
bowhunter, your scouting and hunting are going to be
closely intertwined. It's during the pre-rut that the infor-

Depending on the weather, water can be a critical factor in early fall scouting—but waterholes are always good places to look for sign.

mation you gained during your spring and summer scouting ventures can really pay off. If you've located a big buck or two using a specific feeding area during your late summer scouting and your spring scouting has pinpointed a buck's sanctuary or bedding area, as well as rub lines between the bedding and feeding areas, and loitering or holding areas, your chances of taking a mature buck are excellent. Your best method of attack is to grab a portable treestand, tree steps, and your bow and arrow set and combine your scouting and hunting.

The first step should be to carefully check the most likely approach to the food source for fresh tracks and trails. There will probably be some heavily used trails leading to the feeding area; and while an older mature buck

Preferred foods can change with the seasons, so always be on the lookout for indications of browsing or feeding.

You can find whitetail bucks in the darndest places . . . and you'll often find them where you least expect to. Always keep your eyes open, and don't be afraid to investigate obvious places as well as out-of-the-way hideouts.

will follow the does and fawns onto the feed ground, most wary old-timers usually ease into the territory on a less prominent trail and are likely to move into the open, just at dark or later. When scouting the perimeter of these areas keep your eyes open for lightly used trails and check them for big tracks that will indicate a big deer, more than likely a buck, is using the trail. Cagey older bucks dance to their own tune and as the rut nears they become more and more antisocial and loners. This aloofness can be a blessing in that it's often easier to waylay an unsuspecting lone animal with one set of ears and eyes than one of a group with lots of keen, alert ears and eyes. If you find a likely buck trail, check the wind and move back into the heavy cover, mak-

As hunting season approaches you're better off scouting for night sign on the edges of areas you plan to hunt, saving the core area for the season.

In early fall, high grass as well as standing grain fields are favored places for bucks to hide out.

Rubs will begin to appear well before the rut kicks off proper.

ing sure you stay off the trail and keep the wind in your favor. If there is no way you can enter the woods with the wind in your favor back off and wait for another day. Note the date and wind conditions in your notebook for future references. If you can get back into the cover with the wind in your favor move back100 yards or more while keeping tabs on the buck trail. Hang your treestand with a minimum of disturbance within easy shooting distance of the trail. Be sure you keep the wind in your favor not only for the stand you are hunting but for any of the other trails in the immediate vicinity. A deer winding you and blowing you off will, more than likely, alert any approaching buck and also ruin your chances of surprising him. If you get back in the woods and feel you can't set up over the buck trail without spooking deer approaching on another trail, move to a position where there is no chance of alerting any deer and hang the stand where you can sit and observe the activity and movement patterns during the evening. This information will go a long ways toward putting you in just the right position when the wind is right to hunt the area.

If you do get your stand into position make good use of your binoculars to keep track of what's going on around you at all times. Remember you're scouting as well as hunting. If a trophy buck meanders under your treestand and gives you a good shot, kill him and spend the rest of the season scouting for next year. If you see a good buck using another trail or approach to the feeding areas let him pass. After full dark, sneak quietly out of the area, without alerting or spooking any deer. Return early the next afternoon and move your stand to cover the buck's previous approach path. If you do spook deer in the vicinity, pull out of the area for several days to let things cool down and the deer get back on track before hunting there again. Hope-

The idea of most scouting is to put you in the right place at the right time. This is actually most difficult during the rut, when bucks are extremely unpredictable.

fully the big buck will also settle down and follow the does' lead, but don't bet on it.

If you are going to be scouting during a pre-rut period for a later hunting season, *caution* should be your byword. Be as unobtrusive and careful as possible in all your pre-rut scouting endeavors and move through the area with the same stealth and silence as you would if you were still-hunting. Bumping deer in the area or even bumping a buck from his sanctuary or bedding area once, and then leaving the area undisturbed for a week or more, might not spook them/him into vacating the area. Smearing and splashing copious amounts of scent on the vegetation along trails, and filling the air with the hated man smell and grossly disturbing the area will more than likely put a wary, patriarchal-type buck on the alert at the least and drive him completely out of his core area at the worst. Either way you lose!

What you are looking for in your pre-rut scouting is a fresh line of rubs and scrapes indicating the presence of a mature buck in the area. Along with a number of smaller practice or mock scrapes you should find several much larger primary or signpost scrapes. These are the ones to concentrate your hunting efforts on as the dominant buck in the area is far more likely to check these with regularity than the smaller ones. I've learned the hard way that it's much better to set up on the downwind trails leading to a primary scrape than it is to hunt over the scrape itself. A mature buck will often circle downwind of the scrape to scent, check it rather than move directly to the scrape itself. By setting up 50 to 100 yards downwind of the scrape you may catch the buck as he circles the scrape. If you are gun hunting, 100 yards should be a sure bet. Bowhunters must choose their stand location with much more care and precision than a gun hunter and you may have to carefully move your stand several times to get it into the right location for a good bow shot. If a primary scrape is located in the open it is best to set up on a trail in the dense timber where a cautious buck can observe the scrape without moving into the open. Often such a trail will have a series of rubs along it that might give an indication of the buck's size. A big buck will often rub both large and small diameter trees while smaller bucks will pretty well stick to the smaller shrubs and bushes. Once again it may take several cautious stand relocations to get in just the right position to make the situation produces a trophy buck but that's what scouting is for.

Another key stand location to scout for during the pre-rut period is a loafing or loitering area used by does and fawns as they move from their bedding areas to feeding

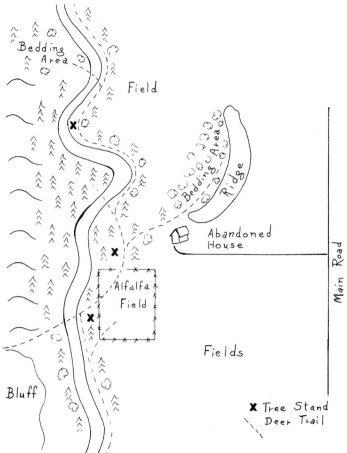

Some areas with limited cover are easy to scout and stand locations stand out like a beacon.

areas. These areas are usually found within a short distance of the food source but usually are in heavy cover where the deer can observe the feeding area and still be in the safety and protection of heavy cover. Usually such an area will have a number of small scrapes and rubs scattered ran-

The problem with the rut is that a hot doe may lead a buck almost anywhere . . . or he may wander almost anywhere in search of a doe.

domly over a sizable area. One such loitering area I found in Iowa last year had 15 scrapes and a dozen rubs within sight of my treestand. Unfortunately I found this spot during the latter part of the rut when the bucks were roaming the countryside in search of does, instead of during the pre-rut when the bucks would have been more likely to check the area frequently in hopes of picking up the scent of a "hot" doe. You can bet I'll be there at the right time this coming fall.

Pre-rut scouting is an important phase in the education of any deer hunter. If you don't succeed in outsmarting a buck during the pre-rut period, add the knowledge and information gained from your scouting to your repertoire of whitetail tactics and make it work for you during the rut.

SCOUTING THE RUT

It's just about impossible to talk about whitetail hunting anytime, anywhere, without the subject of "THE RUT" coming up. The rut is the one period during the year when a trophy buck's instinct for procreation overrides his survival instinct and makes him vulnerable to hunters.

The rut is triggered by the length of the daylight period but weather can and does play an important part in kicking the rut into high gear. In most of the northern two-thirds of the U.S. the peak of the rut will usually fall around the first week in November. In the southern tier of states it can take place anywhere from mid-December through late January. During this period the rutting bucks forsake their core areas or sanctuaries and roam farther and farther afield in search of does in estrus. They use their scrapes much as a fisherman would use a trotline. They keep the scrapes baited (scented), and will keep working them as long as they keep producing does in heat. Once they quit producing for a short time the dominant buck will move on and leave the unproductive series of scrapes to the lesser bucks in the area. The dominant buck will then make a whole new series of scrapes, often in just a couple of hours' time, in another area and start "fishing" again. As the rut progresses the bucks wander farther and farther from their home range or core area and can leave scrapes and rubs scattered from hell to breakfast during their wanderings. A hunter could spend the rest of the season hunting one of these "surefire" locations and never catch a glimpse of the buck that made the scrape.

It's darn hard to distinguish between scouting the rut and hunting the rut. The major difference between scouting and hunting the rut would be whether you were carrying your hunting tools when you were traipsing around the

While rubs appear during the pre-rut, major scrapes are primarily rut sign. And yes, if you scout out a scrape like this, there's a good place for a stand somewhere near.

woods, brush, or fields during the rut. Anyone that is in the field scouting during the rut without the means to shoot a rutting buck is either a nitwit or a guide, or an outfitter with clients. Even when I am hunting during the rut I am also doing some very serious scouting

As an outfitter, it's easy for me to separate my scouting and hunting activities during the rut. When there are

An advantage to the rut, especially for gun hunters, is bucks are more visible than at any other time of the year.

Bill Vaznis put it together on this fine bow-killed whitetail, scouted out and taken during the rut.

Cooney believes in being flexible and covering ground during the rut, checking out new areas especially during the slower midday hours.

clients in camp, neither myself, my partner, nor our guides do any personal hunting. Instead, we spend most of every day during the rut scouting and trying to figure out just how the hell we can get our clients within range of a trophy buck. The unpredictability of bucks during the peak of the rut can often lead to total frustration and a real personal resentment and sense of malice against critters with large antlers and a white tail. During the rut mature bucks may be more visible but that doesn't necessarily mean they're more vulnerable.

This past fall I had carefully and intelligently planned the demise by one of my hunting clients of a trophy buck. I had seen this buck several times previously on a section of property we had leased. There was a long, narrow harvested corn- and bean field that extended from the farm lane to a huge chunk of CRP (Conservation Reserve Program) swamp and chest-high weeds ½ mile north of the lane. The fields were split by a deep tree-lined creek, with steep banks, beaver dams, and bordered on one side by a gravel road that separated the private land from a whole section of prime, public, whitetail habitat. The private land formed a long narrow corridor between the public hunting land and a huge expanse of timbered land where no hunting was allowed, a real deer sanctuary. There were two major deer trails crossing our lease, one by the farm land and another on the upper end, just below the CRP.

Previous to the gun season and rut, I saw several super bucks on both the private and the public land, and I figured on the opening day public land hunters would push deer across our lease to the sanctuary and give one of our clients a chance at them.

In the opening morning darkness I put my gun hunter in a treestand overlooking the upper crossing and drove to the lower crossing to block and observe. As it got light enough to see I picked out the shape of a lone deer in the corn stubble between the road and the creek. As the deer became a distinct shape in the field of my window-mounted spotting scope, I could tell it was definitely a buck. What a buck! By the time it got light enough for good detail, I had a black ring around my eye from jamming it so tightly against the rubber eyepiece. That infernal buck was a perfect 10-point with 12-inch brow tines, 15-inch G-2s 13 to 14-inch G-3s, and 8-inch G-4s. With its mass and length, this majestic rack would have easily scored in the high 170s or low 180s.

There was no way I could get to my client without spooking the buck, so I watched in total frustration as he finally bounded across the road and disappeared into the public land. I figured all was not lost as there was still a possibility he would give my hunter a chance if he tried to cross back into the sanctuary later in the day or if he was spooked by hunters working the public land. Unfortunately, nothing of the kind happened. Such is buck hunting during the rut.

One of our major efforts in scouting during the rut is to locate concentrations of does, usually in or around food sources. Where there are does and fawns the bucks will show up sooner or later. If I find an area where there are a lot of does still with their fawns, indicating they haven't been bred yet, I'll move cautiously into the area during the middle of the day and scout the area for placing a hunter.

With the unpredictability of deer, especially "doe-crazed bucks," during the peak of the rut there is no guarantee you aren't going to jump or spook a bedded deer. During such mid-rut scouting endeavors, I recommend wearing a pair of all-rubber or rubber-bottomed boots to keep your ground scent to a minimum. I spray my rubber boots with a scent eliminator, fox urine or deer urine, just on the off-chance that it will confuse an inquisitive deer's nose and alleviate its suspicions enough to keep it from leaving the area. I never miss a chance to grind my boots in fresh deer droppings or a cow pie for the same reason. I try to move slowly and carefully through the area, staying out of thick brush that will brush up against me and pick up scent. Wearing clean outer garments will help reduce this problem and spraying your clothing with a scent eliminator prior to heading for the woods certainly can't do any harm and will make the product manufacturers happy if nothing else.

I make constant use of my binoculars during such scouting ventures, as my eyes can cover a lot of deer habitat with less fatigue, noise, or scent. It's surprising what you can accomplish with good optics when you learn to use them properly and interpret what you are seeing through them.

Rubs remain productive finds during in-rut scouting, but are more likely to reveal a buck's presence than exactly where he's going to show up.

When scouting an area of known or suspected doe concentrations, I try to find a holding area where the does tend to loiter or hold up during the late morning and early evening before and after feeding. Look for an abundance of tracks, trampled leaves or grass, beds, and droppings. If there are bucks cruising the holding area checking for a doe in estrus, you should find plenty of fresh rubs and scrapes and you might even get a whiff or two of strong,

Aerial photos are the best tool a hunter has for pinpointing travel corridors, crossings, funnel areas, etc. that are vital to good stand location and hunting success.

musky deer smell. If I find an area such as this you can bet I won't be wandering through it and disturbing the scene. Once again I'll depend on my binoculars to help me pick a likely looking tree for a stand if I am contemplating putting a bowhunter in the area, or a suitable ground site if I am going to be bringing a gun hunter to the area. Once I get the lay of the land, check for wind direction, and choose a likely stand location, I'll ease quietly out of the vicinity. On the way I'll select a return route that will take full advantage of the wind direction and is clear of brush and weeds that could brush against us and retain scent. When I return to the area with a client we'll ease quietly into the location with all the essentials and get set up as quickly and quietly with as little disturbance as possible.

For a hunter wanting to be successful at this time of the year, the rut is a time of action and reaction. You observe a buck in action working a doe, or ground signs point to the fact that there are numerous, extremely active deer in the area. If you don't react you are liable to miss your chances at a good buck and maybe the buck of a lifetime. The more aggressively you react during the peak of the rutting activity and the longer you stay in the bush, the better your chances of success. This holds true for both hunting and scouting the rut!

CHAPTER EIGHT

IN-SEASON AND LATE-SEASON SCOUTING

As I've stated throughout this book, scouting is the key to making your hunting season a "lead pipe cinch." All you have to do is spend a couple of days locating a good buck, determine where he is moving during the early morning and late evening hours, slip into his core area, and put up a treestand overlooking one of his travelways. Wait a few days for the season to open and let things quiet down in the woods. Sneak into your stand in the predawn darkness on opening day, and shoot the buck when he comes walking by an hour later. Ohhh! Were it only so easy and assured, I probably wouldn't be writing this chapter or, for that matter, this whole book.

Unfortunately, or fortunately, depending on your perspective, most of us find ourselves still out in the woods well into the season, wondering just how the bloody hell we are going to get a deer close enough to kill, with only a month of the season left. Back to square one . . . SCOUTING!

Early in the season, especially if you're a bowhunter or muzzleloader hunter, you are going to be hunting bucks whose only goals in life are a full belly and lots of undisturbed rest. The only way to take one of these beasties is to pattern them on their way to and from their bedding area. Occasionally, this is a simple process and you can get lucky. Quite often, the largest bucks will simply disappear and

*Always keep your eyes open, not only for deer near your stand, but
also for deer moving near what might be a better stand location.*

In snow country, late-season sign is easy to find. Of course, interpreting *what you see and knowing how to use it are as important as locating the sign itself.*

As cold weather comes on, food becomes increasingly important to deer; feeding areas are prime for both scouting and hunting.

you may never see them again in that particular area. Because of the terrain features, habitat types, or layout of the crops in the area, a mature buck can pull a disappearing act with ease during early fall and the pre-rut.

You may be concentrating your hunting efforts and spending time in a treestand, but never let up on your scouting efforts even when sitting on your butt. During this period of the season you'll probably do most of your hunting early mornings and late evenings, when the reclusive bucks are a bit more active. While you're sitting in the stand, keep your binoculars in action, scouting, especially if you see deer movement. I can't understand how a hunter can sit on any stand or stalk through the woods or prairies without constantly making use of a good set of binoculars. If you see deer moving in the woods or in the open, pinpoint exactly where the deer move through the heavy cover into the feeding area, or cross an open field or disappear into cover, when leaving the feeding ground. As soon as you quit hunting in the morning, when it warms up and the deer have quit moving, leave your stand and spend an hour or two thoroughly scouting the area. If you spot deer in the evening, mark the location in your memory or notebook and return after hunting the following morning. You might be surprised at the unobtrusive and unlikely locations of trails and travel corridors you may have missed on earlier scouting trips, or new ones that weren't active when you scouted the area previously.

If a good buck appears from the same location more than once you had better be carefully scouting for a new stand location, right now! Aggressive and continuous scouting can often make the difference between simply watching deer in frustration, and getting a shot at a buck.

As the season progresses and the farmers and ranchers begin harvesting their crops and reducing vast areas of heavy cover into barren stubble fields in many of the top whitetail areas, there is a drastic change in deer habits. Continual in-season scouting is necessary to keep you constantly aware of current deer locations. This can be a real problem in many areas because the protective cover provided by crops can change on a daily basis. An important part of your in-season scouting should be to stay in contact with locals such as school bus drivers, rural mail carriers, trappers, pheasant hunters, farmers, and ranchers to get the latest input on their deer (especially big buck) sightings.

Another tactic that will give you lots of information on in-season deer movements, whether it is early in the season or during the rut, is what I term "cruise scouting." When I have clients in the field hunting, I cruise the roads in the general area or even a totally new area, concentrating on tracks crossing the road. When I find a likely crossing with lots of sign I scout out the area for hunting potential and check on the landowner status of the adjacent lands. I'll usually brush out all the tracks and make a note of the date in my ever-present notebook. The next time I cruise through the area I'll check the crossing again and if it's still being hammered by deer traffic I'll get serious about finding a place back off the road to locate a stand. This is also an excellent type of location to make use of an electronic trail monitor (see Chapter 3).

This past fall during our pre-season scouting we located a monstrous 150–160 class buck along with several other Pope & Young class bucks that were using a small, overgrown area of hawthorn, sumac, and snowberry as an alternate bedding area. This patch was in the center of a mile-square section and well off the beaten path. It was well hidden at the bottom of a sloping, bowl-shaped depression, bordered by a narrow treeline that separated the bedding ground from several large cornfields.

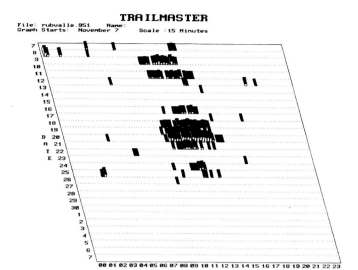

The Trail monitor readout graph on bedding area showing heavy mid-day activity.

Our options for a treestand were limited to one questionable-sized box elder tree on our side of the fence. When we first checked it out and discovered numerous beds and fresh rubs, we mounted an electronic trail monitor to cover the main trail leading into the area along with a portion of the bedding ground. Over a period of a week, the monitor readout showed the deer were moving from the cornfield to the bedding ground around 8:00 or 9:00 a.m. and leaving the patch at 4:00 to 6:00 p.m. on a somewhat sporadic basis. We hunted the patch several times and passed easy shots on some smaller bucks, but the monster never showed. I contacted the owner of the adjacent property to get permission to hunt from the treeline on his property and in our conversation, I found out they were going to pick the adjacent cornfields the following

The author believes in covering ground during midday hours, "cruise scouting," looking for sign as much as for deer.

day. In-season scouting is gathering information any way possible that can help put you in the right place at the right time. By learning of the farmer's upcoming harvest plans, I had a darn good chance to make the most of a promising situation.

The following morning I put one hunter in the brush patch bedding area and another covering a well-used trail along the top of a timbered hillside, bordering the upper end of the cornfield. I told both hunters they were there for the duration of the day or until the combine was done. I figured that sooner or later during the day the combine would get down to the last few rows, and the deer that had been living in the corn all fall would have to vacate and hopefully give one of our hunters a chance.

It's always a good bet to spend some of your in-season scouting checking with farmers as to when they are going to harvest their crops and plan accordingly. I missed a

Gregg Miller with a beautiful late-season whitetail.

record class buck in Illinois several years ago, as he broke out of the last few rows of a field the farmer was picking. The farmer told me he had seen some good bucks in this field and gave me permission to set up on top of a hill where he figured the deer would cross on their way from the field to the nearest heavy woods. Any number of farmers have told me that most deer will simply move over in the field as the combine approaches and normally won't break for the nearest cover until there are only 10 to 20 rows left in the field. Knowing when and how a farmer is going to work his field can give you a great chance to waylay a good buck as he tries to head for the protection of the nearest heavy cover.

By noon the cornfield was about half harvested, so I decided to check on my hunters to find out if they had any activity. The hunter covering the bedding area was totally bored, having seen one pheasant. He was a savvy, trophy whitetail hunter and figured we were on the right track, so he decided to spend the rest of the afternoon in the tree overlooking the bedding ground. The bowhunter guy on which the hill was another story. He could hardly speak when I eased up to his treestand. An hour earlier a monstrous 10-point, the hunter figured would score over 190, had walked out of the corn and stood undecided on the trail he was covering at a distance of 80 yards. The humongous buck then moved along the edge of the cornfield and disappeared 50 yards farther down the ridge, leaving my client in a state of shock. Needless to say, I couldn't have dragged the hunter out of the tree at that point.

When I picked the hunters up at dark-thirty that evening, the hunter on the ridge had passed on a small eight-point. The hunter in the bedding area hadn't seen a thing until 4:00 p.m., when a heavy antlered 10-point that would have scored 160 walked over the hill from the opposite direction and bedded down in the weed patch 75 yards from the treed hunter. The buck was completely hidden in the heavy growth and as far as the hunter was aware the buck was still there when it got dark and I came to pick him up. Sometimes even good information and the best-laid plans don't work when you're dealing with whitetails.

Even with hunting pressure whitetails will generally keep using well-established trails, but they may become more nocturnal so scouting turns to looking for places to ambush them in daylight hours as well as a search for the actual deer.

When pressured, bucks will usually head for the deepest cover, so late-season scouting is often a search for these out-of-the-way hideouts.

When the rut gets in full swing during the season, your best bet is to stay in the woods all day, hunting and scouting or scouting and hunting, whichever works best. The bucks are liable to be anywhere at any time and by staying out or scouting from daylight to dark you are going to increase your chances of an "up-close-and-personal" encounter with one of them.

The main thing to remember during the rut is to be mobile and flexible; don't hunt the same stand or area day in and day out if you aren't seeing bucks. Hunt your favorite stands or areas morning and evening, but cover some new country during the middle of the day, trying to locate a buck on the move. If you see a good buck get after him, either to hunt him right then and there, or scout out the area where you spotted him, trying to find a stand location to hunt from providing, of course, you have permission, or can get it, to hunt the property where you saw the buck.

When you're scouting during the season don't get so over anxious that when you find a "surefire" spot you stop looking. Carefully check the surrounding area for an even better place 'cause there just might be a fresher scrape or rub over the next ridge or a better trail down the next draw.

Failing to follow my own advice probably cost me a 150-class buck several years ago. I had been bowhunting for a week and wasn't seeing the buck I knew was in the area, so I expanded my scouting to take in a stretch of public land I knew harbored a couple of good bucks. The first day I found a well-used, small cornfield that was being worked pretty heavily. I figured to find a location off the field nearer to a bedding area, so I scouted out the section of timber on the ridge above the field. I found lots of rubs along the edge of the woods and a number of scrapes that were being worked. I picked a spot in a corner of the

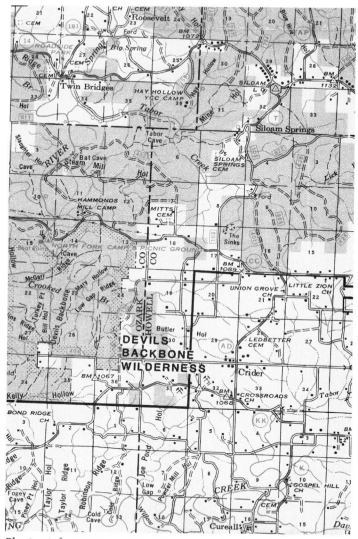

Plotting information on U.S.G.S. maps makes it easier to determine buck activity and travel patterns.

woods overlooking a weed-filled tree plot that looked as if it served a dual purpose as a bedding area and travel corridor between the woods. I was above the field and a more extensive section of timber across the flat. There were five active scrapes along the edge of the woods near the corner, numerous rubs on the young trees in the plot, and several well-used trails emerging from the timber into the weed/tree patch. I stuck up a portable treestand and figured I was going to kill a good buck there in a couple of mornings or evenings . . . Wrong!

I saw several does and a 150-class buck cross the weed patch and enter the timber 75 yards above me but I was so sure I had picked just the right place I didn't bother to check the area into which they crossed. After a few unsuccessful days, I let a friend of mine hunt the stand and he arrowed a doe standing on the scrape just at dark, while he was listening to a buck grunting and raking a tree just behind the stand. The next day, when we went to get the doe, I discovered that the trail past the stand followed the ridge through a small saddle, where a number of small trees had been recently rubbed and thrashed bare, and intersected another trail that paralleled the edge of a deep draw. This well-traveled trail was lined with big rubs and numerous fresh scrapes. It was then obvious the big buck had been sticking to the heavy timber and was simply circling behind my stand on the edge of the open, at least during the daylight hours. The following day I moved the stand to the junction of the trails, but due to business commitments, I never got to hunt the area again. You can bet that's one place I am going to check out this coming fall and you can be sure I am not going to assume that either location where I had the stands last fall is the best place until I thoroughly scout the whole area this time.

There is a narrow line that separates adequate in-season

Judd Cooney with late-season buck taken after glassing him for several days to determine his movements.

scouting to keep you hunting the best areas and your stands in the best locations, from over-scouting that defeats your purpose by driving wary deer out of the area. Only experience and a continual lack of success will tell you when you've crossed this very narrow line.

CHAPTER NINE

POST-SEASON SCOUTING

Yahoo!! Deer season is finally over! You may not have gotten the monster buck you saw 13 times during the season but could never get close to, but what the heck, a tender doe is much better eating than a rank, old, rutting buck anyhow.

Now you can relax, get caught up on your honey do's, get reacquainted with the kids and completely forget about deer hunting until a couple of days before the season next fall. Wrong! Sure you can relax, do your wife's bidding, and hold those kids on your lap during cartoons on TV, but you're a dang fool or a very naive deer hunter if you don't take advantage of the best scouting time of the year.

With the recently past hunting season still a vivid memory, along with the highs and lows of your hunting experiences, you can head into your hunting area or scout new locations without the pressure of needing to maximize your valuable time by spending every minute hunting. Now you can take your time and scout various areas of intrigue without worrying about spooking deer, leaving scent, or disturbing the area enough to scare a suspicious buck completely out of the country.

Actually, you can even sneak into such areas and purposely jump the bucks out of their sanctuaries, so you can get visual confirmation of their size and trophy qualities. This "near-hunting" activity will give you good practical

Post-season scouting is probably the nearest thing to the hunting season; the deer haven't moved much from their in-season haunts, so there is much to be learned.

experience and also give you information on particular bucks that survived all the previous seasons and will, in all probability, be using the same areas again the next fall.

Hunting post-season bucks with a camera is also another way to extend your hunting season, further your whitetail education, and record some of the bucks in your hunting spot on film for posterity. Spooking bucks out of their retreats at this time of year shouldn't affect their return in the slightest.

If your hunting area doesn't get inundated by snow during the post-season, you'll still be able to see scrapes and rubs made during the rut. Post-season scouting is the only time you can thoroughly scout an area for fresh rubs and scrapes when the season isn't on and you don't have to worry about spooking the quarry you're trying to get close to.

By starting at known feeding grounds, you can carefully work the area, scouting for faint buck trails, scrape lines, and rub lines. When you locate a good trail or rub line you have the freedom to follow it, hoping to find a staging area or buck bedding area. When you find a buck's sanctuary you can spend all the time it takes to thoroughly scout every nook and cranny of his hidey-hole. Locate and back-track every trail leading to the bedding ground, keeping an eye open for traditional scrapes and rubs also called "sign-post" rubs. A buck will return to these rubs and scrapes each year and on a regular basis during the rut. Locating a good stand site near one of these permanent, traditional rubs and/or scrapes is like making a deposit in the bank. Take the time to choose a route to your future stand location that minimizes the chances of a bedded buck hearing, smelling, or seeing your approach.

During all your scouting ventures, take notes on what you found where, and mark key features, buck sightings, and stand locations on a U.S.G.S. map or aerial photo for future study. If you are really serious about your scouting, and you darn sure should be, you might consider using one of the high tech GPS (Global Positioning System) units to mark the location of your finds. It's a simple matter to punch a button and mark a stand site or traditional scrape as a waypoint in your GPS unit. At present a GPS will get you to within a maximum of 100 yards of any waypoint and that distance will be dropped to mere feet within a short time due to recent changes in government restrictions. In years to come, more and more avid deer hunters are going to be making use of GPS units in their scouting endeavors and there's no reason you shouldn't start now.

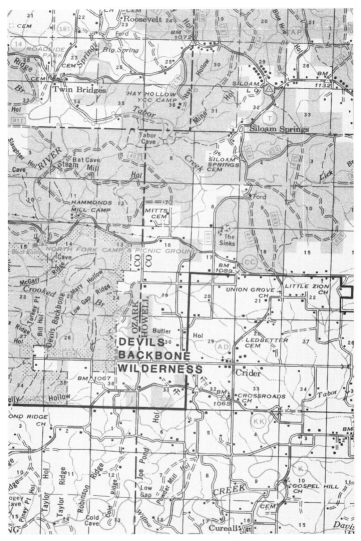

Enlarged section of U.S.G.S. map is ideal for locating post-season scouting information.

Post-season is a particularly good time to learn which bucks have survived the season, especially in the period after they settle down and before they begin to shed antlers.

If you are in a state or province where the use of bait or feeders is legal, the post-season is the time to locate areas where you can take a trophy buck. Wary, mature, record-class bucks are rarely taken on feeders or bait piles that are regularly hunted during the season. I've talked with a number of hunters that have sat over baited areas day in and day out, without seeing a really big buck in the area. Yet, when they scout the area for antlers in the spring, they find several sets of sheds that would make any hunter drool with anticipation.

A close friend of mine owns a 1,000-acre high-fenced ranch, where the Hill Country and South Texas meet. Most of the fenced area is covered with heavy stands of cedar that make for ideal deer habitat. The fenced area has numerous year-round feeders scattered around it and permanent towers overlooking every feeder. The owner is heavily into trophy deer management and works hard at maintaining a quality deer herd. The ranch is hunted steadily from opening to closing day of the season and yet when the ranch manager makes post-season helicopter counts, he always finds a number of record-book bucks that nobody sees during the rest of the year, proof positive that big bucks learn to avoid daylight appearances around feeders.

For my money a feeder is great for attracting does, fawns, and small bucks and creating trails I can follow away from the feeder or bait station to locate an area where I can set up on a trophy buck.

Post-season is an ideal time to backtrack the trails leading to a baited area looking for a key staging area, where the does and young bucks congregate before moving out to feed. A high incidence of fresh rubs and scrapes or pawed, up dirt in the area is a good indication of the buck activity during the previous rut. A number of large, rubbed trees should make your mouth water in anticipation of the coming season and rut period, when you can be sitting in a treestand, hunting the area. Much like a staging or loitering area in the heavy timber near a cornfield or alfalfa patch, these areas are ideal places during the rut for ambushing a buck that's checking the area for a "hot" doe.

These staging areas may only be a hundred yards from the bait station if the surrounding cover is thick, dense woodland; or they may be a half mile or more away in relatively open brush or cedar country.

If your hunting area is in snow country, post-season is a perfect time to backtrack the trails leading to a feeder or bait pile to find one of these areas. You don't have to stop with the locating of a holding area. You can continue on the trail scouting for intersecting trails, bedding areas, travel corridors between different habitat types, and any other situation that can put you close to a deer during the season.

Generally by the time deer season is over, all crops are out of the fields and the ground is either stiff or frozen harder than a rock and the area farmers and ranchers are more inclined to grant you permission to drive on their fields, meadows and pastures. This gives you a chance to cover a lot of country in short order in your post-season scouting. Drive the edges of the fields and pastures checking for active trails and note them for future reference. Make it a point to check isolated thickets of brush, patches of weeds, cattail-clogged sloughs, or small brush-filled tree belts. These areas are ideal escape cover for a smart, old buck that has been pressured out of his core area by hunters. A trophy buck may well spend the entire season in just such a small parcel of cover, if he is not disturbed, venturing out to feed only at night. During the rut, the buck may well move out after dark, locate a receptive doe, and herd her back into his sanctuary for breeding. Check

Winter starts to concentrate deer around available food sources, and in snow country they tend to yard up so their collective feet can paw through the snow. Both are good conditions for seeing what kind of deer herd exists.

John Sloan with a fine muzzleloader buck. Taking a buck like this is the ultimate goal of all scouting, regardless of what time of year.

every likely looking thicket you come across in your post-season scouting. If you find one with deer beds that looks like it has been harboring a buck for quite some time, check the surrounding area for approach routes with the wind in your favor and try to find a location where you can use binoculars and spotting scope to glass the area. Mark this spot on your map or aerial photo for serious consideration late in next year's season.

There's a sure way to add some excitement to your post-season scouting that will benefit the deer in your area and possibly open some new hunting areas for you to scout. Every state and province where I've hunted whitetails the past 10 years has been inundated with coyotes. In a number of states and several of the Canadian provinces, the rapidly multiplying coyote population is making serious inroads into the whitetail population and their fawn populations are taking a beating each year.

You can bet where you find deer you'll find coyotes and vice versa. I can recall a number of times where a set of coyote tracks has led me into a deer "honey hole" I didn't know existed or had been bypassing because it just didn't fit my concept of a holding area for deer. Coyotes are master predators and you can learn a lot about hunting by following a set of coyote tracks in the snow as he tries to find a warm body to convert to coyote crap.

Combining your post-season scouting efforts with some serious predator hunting can often provide an opportunity to scout fresh country and give you a solid reason to make contact with ranchers and farmers. Over the years I have obtained permission to hunt a lot of country by getting acquainted with landowners and helping to alleviate some of their predator problems. You can thoroughly scout an area while you are hunting or calling predators and easily determine its hunting potential for the future. Don't hesitate to ask the landowner or his children to accompany you on your scouting/hunting trip. Developing a good solid friendship is by far the best way to get permission for deer hunting, and post-season predator hunting-scouting junkets can certainly open that window of opportunity.

Post-season scouting is the very best way to start preparing for the deer season next fall and extending your time in the woods after the present season. You can rest assured that your post-season efforts are going to be repaid many times over when the fall while deer season rolls around. Your post-season scouting efforts will go a long way toward increasing your chances of putting yourself in the same place at the same time as a wary, mature buck during the following fall hunting season.

CHAPTER TEN

SCOUTING TO SUCCESS

As I have stated throughout this book, scouting is a year-round endeavor that takes place before, during, and after the hunting season. Aggressive scouting and utilizing the knowledge gained can often make the difference between the success or failure of your whitetail hunt or taking a trophy buck rather than just another deer.

This fact was driven home to me for the umpteenth time just this past week during an early September bowhunt in northern Montana. This hunt was set up by Bill Jordan, designer of Realtree camouflage, and his right-hand man, David Blanton. The main group of bowhunters would be hunting the grain and alfalfa fields along the famous Milk River on a series of adjoining ranches that had been under trophy deer management for several years. These ranches were producing some impressive whitetail bucks and equally awe-inspiring numbers of deer. Harold Knight of Knight and Hale Game Calls, an equally avid bowhunter, and I would be bowhunting another ranch, on the well-known Frenchman Creek, with outfitter Don Lynn, owner of Montana Breaks Outfitters of Malta, Montana. Don has been in the outfitting business for 10 years, concentrating mainly on mule deer and elk. This was his first year at serious whitetail outfitting for bowhunters but he was enthusiastic and had been doing his homework and scouting.

Don had leased a mile section of land along Frenchman

Transitional feeding patterns during early seasons can drive one to drink but constant scouting can bring success.

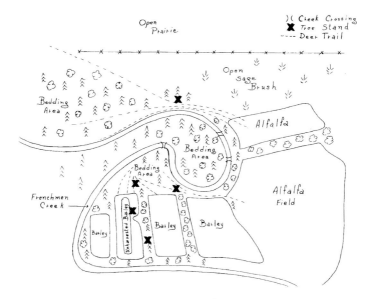

Whitetail habitat along Frenchmen Creek.

Creek that had a super population of whitetails including some real wallhangers. This choice chunk of prime western whitetail habitat consisted of a series of native hay, lush irrigated alfalfa, and barley field,s surrounded by dense brush, impenetrable willow thickets, and head-high grass and brush, interspersed with cottonwood, elm, and alder groves. The country surrounding the half-mile wide river bottom is open, barren, rolling hills covered with sparse sagebrush and coarse prairie grasses. The major portion of the whitetail population is concentrated along the river bottom while the muleys roam the open prairies above.

Don, along with head guide Eric Korman, had spent a number of mornings and evenings scouting and glassing the alfalfa and barley fields along the creek bottom, pinpointing the location of some of the larger bucks and noting their entrance and exit routes from the bedding areas in the creek bottom. Once they had figured out where the bigger bucks were moving from the bedding areas to the feeding fields, they went in during the middle of the day and put up a couple of treestands to accommodate Harold and me for our hunt.

With the preferred whitetail habitat limited to the confines of the river and creek bottoms of Montana many deer populations tend to be very concentrated with a lot of deer moving, feeding, and bedding in a small area. This high concentration of animals makes on-the-ground scouting and moving around the river bottoms, without spooking deer and alerting wary bucks to the intrusion and putting them on full alert, a tough proposition.

The evening we arrived, Harold, Don, and I drove to some high ridges a half-mile above the river bottom, overlooking the area we were to hunt the following evening. In the hour before darkness we glassed over a hundred head of deer feeding in the alfalfa and barley fields. All of the deer on the eastern edge of the river bottom, where Harold's perch for the following evening was located passed on the heavily used trails within bow range of his treestand. The distance and fading light made it impossible to see just where the deer were emerging on the far side of the field, where I would be waiting in ambush the next evening, but the sheer number of deer appearing in an endless procession out of the brush definitely got our adrenaline rates soaring.

The battle plan on all the ranch properties was to confine our hunts to evenings only. Getting into the areas for a morning hunt without spooking or alerting the deer was almost an impossibility, especially where Harold and I were going to be hunting. The first evening, Don dropped Harold and one of Bill's cameramen off near his treestand

Making use of binoculars can make a difference even during the hunt.

Glassing and figuring out what a deer is going to do before he does it are the key to a successful hunt.

in a gnarled old cottonwood at the outside curve of the meandering creek. All the trails leading from the brushy bedding areas, scattered for half a mile up the creek, merged into one major deer travel corridor twenty yards out from the cottonwood.

My stand was situated fifteen feet up another cottonwood thirty yards in from the edge of a barley field where the barley had been cut and windrowed just a couple of days earlier. The stand overlooked a well-used trail down a narrow funnel of cover between the steep creek bank and the edge of the barley field that led to the outer perimeter of a green alfalfa field. An ideal setup.

At 6:20 p.m. a doe and fawn sauntered under my stand and gave me a chance to practice drawing a time or two. At

The only way to take a buck like this is to stay one step ahead of him.

It's great when a plan comes together.

Judd Cooney with a Pope & Young buck.

6:40 a P&Y 8-point buck appeared, moving slowly through the heavy grass and brush 50 yards above my stand. I watched as he moved out of the trees and into another small barley field 100 yards from me and started munching barley heads. I had only given the field a cursory glance through the trees but with my glasses on the feeding buck I could plainly see there was a thirty-yard strip of barley still standing. Over the next couple of hours I watched deer after deer moving to and from that strip of uncut barley. Unfortunately none of them came under my treestand. It was obvious that the deer had changed their travel patterns. When Don and Eric had glassed the uncut barley fields the deer were using the barley and alfalfa with equal gusto and traveling the trail under the treestand to get to both feeding areas. All might have stayed equal if the rancher had cut all the barley but by leaving a narrow strip of standing grain to tantalize and attract the deer he had totally changed their travel patterns.

Rather than being dejected when Don picked me up that night, I was hyped! I couldn't wait until the midday lull the next day so we could get back and confirm what my treestand scouting had indicated. The little patch of uncut barley would concentrate the deer in a smaller area and just might draw a big buck within bow range. The following day Don and I circled the barley field several times in his pickup, checking trails, tracks, and wind direction before I picked a spot for my stand. The end of the field adjacent to the thick brush and woods had five beaten-down trails emerging within the fifty-yard width of the field and would have made an excellent stand location, but a westerly wind would have been blowing scent back into the bedding area. I finally put up a fourteen-foot ladder stand near the center of a strip of trees separating two of the barley patches where I saw a number of deer moving between the

Judd setting up a treestand on his Montana hunt.

Judd in a treestand during his Montana hunt.

fields. The predicted northwest wind would be carrying my scent over the least likely travel area for approaching deer and with the sun heating the field all day there was a good chance the thermal updraft from the warm ground during the cool evening would carry my scent up and out of reach of any nearby deer.

By 5:00 o'clock that evening I was comfortably situated in my stand and ready for action. The first little buck ran into the field at 6:00 and literally attacked the standing barley. From that point until dark there was a constant stream of deer moving into the field and past my stand. At one time there were twenty deer in the field feeding with nine bucks ranging from spikes to a wide-antlered 9-point that would have easily made P&Y. The larger buck, still in full velvet, fed to within fifteen yards of my stand and posed broadside for five minutes before moving off. I passed, hoping for a bigger buck and knowing that this hot spot was going to do nothing but get better. By dark it was obvious I needed to move my stand another fifty yards toward the end of the field into a huge cottonwood on a small point that protruded out into the field. Some of the deer were feeding up to that point and then meandering through the trees into the adjacent fields. From my present stand I couldn't see the end of the field around the corner from the big cottonwoods and figured I might be missing some deer. From the cottonwood I could cover the whole lower end of the field and also any deer that tried to move around the point.

Several of the hunters in camp had killed good bucks that evening, so the following day, Realtree's Mike Waddell, Don, and I returned to the field at midday and moved the stand again. As with almost any whitetail hunt, just about the time you think you are getting ahead of the game and gaining an advantage, along comes something or somebody to upset the apple cart. In this case it was the rancher driving his trusty windrower. Had this been my lease I would have already made arrangements with the landowner to leave a portion of the field as a food plot. This was a tactic unfamiliar to Don and he didn't feel that he wanted to press the issue with the rancher right at that moment. By the time the rancher was finished with the small plot of barley we had our double stands in place and left to wait for evening. I figured the deer would return in numbers again that night since they were programmed to the standing barley but once they found the barley cut they would start spreading out again.

By dark that evening I could have arrowed a number of smaller bucks in the 100–125 class and had seen one good buck in the 150 class on the far side of the creek and figured we would give that stand one more evening on the off chance the big buck would move across the creek and join the 25 or so deer we had observed. When Don left earlier in the afternoon, he jokingly pointed out a 3'-by-10' patch of uncut barley that the farmer had missed behind a dirt bank and stated, "See, he did leave you a food plot!" Every deer that came into the cut field that night ended up spending a few minutes munching in that small patch and presented me with a good shot. Don't overlook SMALL patches of choice feed, because the deer darn sure won't.

The following afternoon found Michael and me back in the same stand once again but I didn't have very high hopes of lots of four-footed company. Since the barley fields were now all down and windrowed there was nothing special to hold the deer in our field or bring them past my stand. I was right! That evening we had one buck come within bow range of the stand and although we saw about the same number of deer they simply scattered throughout the field we were watching and into the adjoining fields. A

A couple of small whitetail bucks still in velvet.

few minutes before final shooting light faded a very nice buck in the 130–140 class stepped out of the brush at the end of the field and worked his way along the edge of an irrigation ditch 50 yards across the field. He was a heavy-beamed 8-point with long tines and perfectly matched rack that I would have arrowed in a heartbeat had he been a bit closer and in better light. His appearance left no doubt about where I was going to move the stand for the last evening of my bowhunt.

The following afternoon Mike, Don, and I once again pulled the stands and moved to the end of the field. I eased into the heavy grass, brush, and trees and carefully reconned the area for our last stand. Fortunately the wind had shifted to the south and southeast, which gave us a lot more leeway in choosing a stand site. One heavily used trail snaked along the bank of the creek that paralleled the bedding area for several hundred yards awhile the most heavily used trail was about 40 yards farther into the brush. As the main trails approached the field they forked and re-forked into numerous small trails. I found a suitable cottonwood right on top of the most heavily trodden trail where I could cover the two main trails and still have a pretty decent shot at any deer passing through the brush to the south of me. The southeast wind would give me a good shot at any passing deer before they had even a slight chance of winding us.

Both Michael and I had worn Scent-Loc suits under our Realtree Extra camo to help keep our scent to a minimum. I had also sprayed the area around the base of the tree with Robinson's scent eliminator spray. I don't think anything will completely eliminate or cover human scent under hunting conditions but even if our precautions only diluted our scent a bit it was worth the effort.

From 6:30 that evening on, it seemed there was always a deer or two in sight and several small bucks passed within easy bow range on both sides of the stand. The same wide-antlered 9-point and two does appeared, moving down the trail along the creek and somehow picked up a trace of scent on the wind. They showed alarm but bounded back the way they came without blowing and making a lot of racket. A few minutes later another 9-point came down the main trail and ended up right at the base of the ladder stand for five minutes, checking out all the strange smells before he joined a couple of passing does and headed for the fields. It was fast approaching quitting time and the end of my Montana hunt when I spotted a buck coming out of a thicket 100 yards up the trail. I eased my bow into position for a shot and then saw that he was just a basket-racked 8-point. He veered off the trail and paused broadside at 25 yards but I only caught that out of the corner of my eye as I had picked up a movement where he had appeared a few minutes earlier. Immediately caught the white flash of antlers, BIG ANTLERS! I hissed to catch Mike's attention and when I turned back the buck was coming at a trot. He veered off the trail at the same point as the smaller buck and when he emerged from under the drooping branches of a low-growing cottonwood and I got a good look at his high rack, there was no doubt about my taking the shot. I jerked my 83# Bear Majestic XLR to full draw and was about to halt the buck with a grunt when he stopped in the same spot as the smaller buck. My concentration was already centered on his rib cage and the second he came to a stop my arrow was in flight. There was a flat smack and the buck was gone.

I don't believe in waiting the standard 30 minutes because all that does is give an animal time to start recovering so I unsnapped my safety belt and was on the ground with my bow in less than a minute. The 10-point 140-class buck had made it through a small opening in the brush and was down for the count less than 15 yards from where my Phantom-tipped Easton 2613 had slammed into him.

Now that's the way to end a hunt! If I had just sat in my treestand enjoying the scenery and patiently waiting for a big buck to wander my way, I doubt if I would have come off this hunt with anything more than memories. By keeping my eyes open (scouting) and constantly trying to figure what the deer were doing and why, I was able to move into position where I was in the same place at the same time as a record-book buck. It may have only been for the total of a single minute or two over a period of five days, but it was long enough to take a trophy buck and that's the name of the game.

INDEX

Bold page numbers indicate photos or illustrations.

scouting
  aggressive, 151-67
  cruise, 126
  definition of, 5, 9-10
  electronic, 38-51
  horseback, 31
  hunting and, 8-11, 70-81,
    98-99, 148-49
  post-season, 139-49
  pre-rut, 97-109
  pure-form, 10
  rut, 110-19
  season, 121-37
  springtime, 69-83
  summertime, 85-95
  theory of, 5-11
  from vehicle, 25-26, 29-31,
    145, 148
  wind, 53-67
  scrapes
  pre-rut, 97-98, 107
  rut, 110, **111**
signpost, 107, 141
Sloan, John, **147**
  timer, trail, **33, 40,** 40-42
string, 40-41
tracks, **77**
trails, 74, 76-78, **131**
  bedding area, 82-83, 121,
    125, **153**
  feeding area, 22, 97-99,
    101, **153**

  monitoring, **33, 40,** 40-51,
    45
treestand
  location of, **74,** 89, 107-9,
    108
  observation, 90-91
  wind and, 54, 60
turkeys, 70-78
U.S. Department of Agricul-
    ture, 19
U.S. Geological Survey Infor-
    mation Services Office,
    14, 16
Vaznis, Bill, **113**
vehicles, four-wheel-drive
  damage from, 26, 29
  scouting from, 25-26,
    29-31, 145, 148
Waddell, Mike, **71,** 163-67
Wadsworth, Ron, **61**
waterholes, 86, 88-89
  pre-rut scouting of, 97-98
wind
  bowhunting and, 58-67
  human scent in, 53-55
  movement, 53-55, 57-78,
    60-67
  stand location and, 54, 60
  terrain effect on, 53-55